THE MAKING OF A
LEGACY

Copyright © 2025 by Floyd C. Davis

Published by Arrows and Stones

All rights reserved. No portion of this book may be reproduced, stored in a retrieval system, or transmitted in any form or by any means—electronic, mechanical, photocopy, recording, scanning, or other—except for brief quotations in critical reviews or articles, without prior written permission of the author.

Scripture quotations are taken from the Holy Bible, New International Version®, NIV®. Copyright © 1973, 1978, 1984, 2011 by Biblica, Inc.™ Used by permission of Zondervan. All rights reserved worldwide. www.zondervan.com. The "NIV" and "New International Version" are trademarks registered in the United States Patent and Trademark Office by Biblica, Inc.™

For foreign and subsidiary rights, contact the author.

Cover design by Sara Young

ISBN: 978-1-964794-78-5   1 2 3 4 5 6 7 8 9 10
Printed in the United States of America

THE MAKING OF A
LEGACY

THE REMARKABLE LIFE OF FLOYD C. DAVIS

ARROWS & STONES

To my beautiful bride, Angela, my friend, my love who was always my greatest supporter and a profound inspiration.

Contents

PREFACE	Who Is Floyd C. Davis?	9
CHAPTER 1.	Against Great Odds	13
CHAPTER 2.	Hard Times and Heritage	19
CHAPTER 3.	Out on My Own	29
CHAPTER 4.	Building a Foundation on the Working Road	37
CHAPTER 5.	True Grit and Drive	53
CHAPTER 6.	Satellite Businesses	71
CHAPTER 7.	The BIG One	83
CHAPTER 8.	Vendor of the Year	97
CHAPTER 9.	Small Town Bank and Real Estate	109
CHAPTER 10.	A Chat With Lewis Beavers	119
CHAPTER 11.	Heart of Gold	129
CHAPTER 12.	The Love Story	137
CHAPTER 13.	Love for a Father	157
CHAPTER 14.	Words From Crystal	199
EPILOGUE	Floyd C. Davis Quotes and Thoughts	207
	About the Ghost Author	213

PREFACE

WHO IS FLOYD C. DAVIS?

As you picked up this book, you may have asked yourself this very question. And as you begin to turn the following pages, you may wonder, *Why would I want to read a book about a man I do not know?*

The answer, both mysterious and obvious, is that we all desire connection. Everyone loves a good, captivating story. Storytelling is a fundamental part of our human expression and has a profound impact on how we perceive and understand the world around us. The stories we share help us make sense of our experiences, connect us with others, and create a shared sense of meaning and understanding. Through storytelling, we can grow, be inspired, and oftentimes find parts of ourselves written in another's story.

To answer your lingering question, "Who is Floyd C. Davis?" I'll start with this.

Floyd C. Davis is a man of true grit and drive! A man driven for better. Driven to move forward. Driven to give birth to an idea. A man driven to dream the impossible, to overcome every obstacle and challenge. A man of persistence. A man of perseverance. A man filled with passion. A man who has faced obstacles fearlessly. A man of strong character, work ethic, and motivation.

Floyd was an entrepreneur before it was trendy. He is a man with a great measure of faith. A humble visionary with very humble beginnings. A risk taker. A family man. A hard-working man unafraid of getting his hands dirty. A provider for his family and a giver to those in need, friend and stranger alike. A kind man. Businessman. Banker. Fun-loving. Dancer. Successful. Fearless. A man of tenacity. A man of resilience. Courageous. Determined.

In the following pages detailing Floyd's journey, you'll find that some of these qualities have been shaped and refined over the years, while others appear to be innate, a God-given gift from the start. Together, they have molded him and served him well.

The term "true grit" refers to the quality of perseverance and determination in the face of challenges or obstacles. It means having the strength of character to keep going, working hard, and staying focused on a goal, even when things get tough. As you begin to read his story, you'll discover that from his humble beginnings, Floyd has been grounded in "true grit."

"Drive" refers to a strong motivation or ambition to achieve something. It is the inner force that propels us forward, pushes us to take action, and keeps us committed to our objectives. Drive is often fueled by passion, purpose, or a desire for success. I cannot better describe the "drive" Floyd possesses.

Both true grit and drive are important qualities that can lead to personal growth, success, and the accomplishment of goals. They involve a strong work ethic, resilience in the face of setbacks, and a persisting positive mindset. This is Floyd Davis.

As a man of faith, Floyd exhibits the virtue of steadfastness found in 1 Corinthians 15:58:

> *"Therefore, my dear brothers and sisters, stand firm. Let nothing move you."*

He embodies the character of endurance described in Luke 21:19:

> *"Stand firm, and you will win life."*

They say time travel is not possible. I beg to differ. I had the distinct honor of sharing a cup of coffee with the local legend as he led me through the corridors of time—the last eighty-five years of his life.

It has also been said that nothing will come from nothing. On this, too, I beg to differ, and as you begin to read the following pages that contain only glimpses into the life of this local legend, I believe you also will conclude that you can:

> *"Make anything with grit and drive alone."*
> —Floyd Calvin Davis, Sr.

True grit and drive are bound together, creating this massive unstoppable force—this is Floyd C. Davis.

So, who is Floyd C. Davis? Simple.

A legacy builder.

Curious? Let's dive in, and let his story reveal the rest.

CHAPTER 1

Against Great Odds

Born in December of 1937, Floyd C. Davis began his life amid one of the toughest decades—the 1930s—right in the middle of the Great Depression. These struggles forced many out of their original home communities to search for work and provision. It was for this very reason that the Davis family settled in Atlanta, Georgia, in hopes of finding a more promising life. So, the rugged downtown streets of Atlanta in Fulton County would be his first childhood home.

The Great Depression had taken a toll on the entire country's economy. Many people lost their jobs, homes, land, and possessions, and Atlanta was no exception. Georgia suffered crop failures because of a boll weevil infestation and faced a great drought. Many farmers struggled to keep their land. The Georgia cotton-based economy and agriculture of the South were hit hard.

HANGING DOG, NORTH CAROLINA

Joseph McKinley Davis, Floyd's father, was born in 1899 in the foothill community of Hanging Dog, North Carolina, near Murphy. Joe, as he was called, provided for his family by driving oxen-pulled wagons of logs to a local sawmill. He was not an educated man, so his work consisted of common labor jobs.

Floyd's memories of his dad are very few. When he was just a young toddler, Floyd's dad left the family for reasons unknown. Floyd's entire life has been underscored with these thoughts about his dad:

I never really knew him.

I couldn't tell you much about my dad because he left my mama early in my life. I can remember one thing my brothers and sisters told me about him—he moved from one job to the next, working common labor jobs.

I don't remember much about him, his family, or background. He left and wasn't in my life.

These words were not easy for Floyd to admit, but he spoke them with an air of acceptance that the years and distance had forged within him, mixed with a hint of buried hurt and pain.

Hanging Dog is a small community in Cherokee County. The name of the area was believed to have originated from a legend—a story about a young Cherokee Indian and his hunting dog, Wolf. The tale has it that during a long cold winter, while out tracking a large buck, Wolf and the young Cherokee Indian hunter barely escaped after getting hung up in a large mass of jammed logs and vines from a flash-flooded creek. The story recounts how the brave Indian hunter rescued his dog from the jammed logs in the bitter ice-cold waters, and they both returned to their village with the successful kill—the large buck—after overcoming great odds in their hunting pursuit.

Early settlers found deposits of iron in Hanging Dog, and it became the economic resource of the area. The smelting process of iron used at this time required furnace temperatures beyond melting point and the use of large amounts of wood and charcoal. It is believed Joe's work also included driving oxen-pulled wagons of logs and charcoal to the furnaces.

Floyd's birth order in the Davis family placed him as the youngest of eight children. Floyd had four half-siblings: three half-sisters, Bertha Mae, Stella, and Eula Belle, and one half-brother, James. He also had three natural siblings—Louise, Mack, and Clyde.

His older siblings lost their mother due to a battle with tuberculosis, leaving his dad a widower with four children. Soon after their mother's death, Social Services placed the four children in an orphanage in North Carolina where they remained until Floyd's father remarried. Another family adopted James.

While Floyd's memory of how his dad and mother met eluded him, he was confident to note that his mother, Roxie Lunsford, was only thirteen years old when she married his dad.

"They were married in Heflin, Alabama, because they were of legal age; thirteen years old was the age you could marry in Alabama at the time," Floyd recalls.

Roxie and Joe were married by a justice of the peace in Heflin, and as a young bride, Roxie was instantly placed in the role of mother to Floyd's half-sisters. Roxie, too, was born in Hanging Dog, but in 1910. While it is not known how Floyd's mother and father met, he is both certain and proud of his Hanging Dog heritage.

Not long after Joe and Roxie married, Joe moved the family from the North Carolina foothill community of Hanging Dog to Atlanta. It was here the family began to grow with the births of Louise, Mack, Clyde, and Floyd.

Roxie and Joe also had two other children who both died very young: Jewel Josephine, who died around age one, and Lena Lorene, who did not make it to her first birthday. This meant that Roxie, as a young girl and wife, gave birth to a total of six children.

Roxie with Belle, Louise, Mack, Clyde, and Floyd

In 1937, Roxie, now close to twenty-eight years old, brought Floyd into the world by natural childbirth at home in their Atlanta house. While she had no complications during the home birth, her newborn son developed pneumonia, and it threatened his early life.

Floyd recalls: "The landmark Grady Hospital in Atlanta was instrumental in saving my life. While I don't remember much about those early days, my mama did tell me it was quite a scare having to leave your newborn at the hospital."

It was at Grady Hospital that the infant Floyd received his medical care in overcoming one of the first obstacles of his life.

As the stories began to roll out of this man's heart, I couldn't help but understand the providential heritage Floyd has. He grew up without a father in his life. His family was from a small community with such an incredible story of overcoming great odds. He was born during an era of hardship, struggles, shattered economy and unfavorable odds, and in his first days of life, he overcame the threat of pneumonia.

Such great odds stacked against him foretell the compelling story of "A Man From Hanging Dog: The Floyd C. Davis Story." It is one man's life journey from poor-poor to a "Man of Millions."

Floyd in his toddler years

CHAPTER 2

Hard Times and Heritage

With a fresh cup of coffee in hand, Floyd began to recall his early childhood years.

"Times were hard back then. We didn't know how hard we had it. We just knew there was Mama and all us young'uns trying to make it somehow.

"My dad had troubles with alcohol, and early in my life, Dad left Mama to raise all of us by herself."

Waves of emotions welled up from deep within this stoic, humble man as he began to reveal the impact of those hard days and tough times. He recounted a story of how the times were so hard and tight that the family bathed only once a week, and being the youngest meant he was last to get his turn in the "bath water."

"By the time I got my turn to bathe, that water was murky and dirty, and it didn't smell good either.

"I knew my brothers had purposely peed in the water, and I refused to wash my face," He continued the story.

"One day, while playing with my best buddy, he told me, 'My mama says I can't play with you anymore.' When I asked him why, he said, 'Because you's dirty.'"

Holding the tears at bay, this eighty-five-year-old man, standing tall, full of years of experience, wisdom, and endless grit and drive, squared off with a flood of feelings and emotions. His determination, evident in everything he has accomplished in his life, was now once again unveiled as he swallowed a sip of his coffee and jumped right back into his stories.

While the early years bore scars of tough times, Floyd always held a precious, proud heritage. Floyd's face lit up when he told of a recent road trip where he took some of his grandkids back to Hanging Dog. You could see the joy on his face that this trip brought him as he shared his family's birthplace and stomping grounds from his younger days with his grandkids.

"I took several of my grandchildren on a trip back to my roots in Hanging Dog and Frog Holler recently. I felt it was important for them to see where I had come from, and also where their roots ran deep in the North Carolina foothills, our ancestry, and our connections to the Indians.

"We visited some of the very places my family lived, like the creek. They got to see how hard it was growing up with not much but dirt floors and no indoor plumbing.

"I wanted them to understand where I had come from, the hard times I had faced early in life living dirt poor, and I wanted them to experience the beautiful country of Hanging Dog and Frog Holler that I experienced as a young child."

Floyd was around three years old when his dad left his mother to raise the remaining seven children still living at home. It was speculated that his dad's love for alcohol eventually led him to divorce Roxie and pursue other women. The divorce was a difficult time for his mother, but Floyd remembered how special his mother was.

"My mama was always tough. I learned a lot from her about tough love. She did everything she could to make sure we kids got to eat. It might not have been much—maybe just potatoes or soup—but she made sure we didn't go too hungry, and she taught us early responsibilities, chores and helping each other out. Each of us kids learned to do our part."

Local street signs in Hanging Dog community reflecting the Davis family heritage

CALHOUN, GEORGIA

Floyd remembers when his mother moved the family from Atlanta to Calhoun, Georgia, to begin working at Chenille Bedding Factory when he was about four years old. While he says he doesn't recall much about the move, he does know his mom was in search of work, so she could afford to raise him and his brothers and sisters. Factory work was hard with long hours, but that was where the jobs were. Calhoun was a strong leader in the textile industry, and securing a job would help his mother to raise her children alone.

Floyd recalls:

"She worked at Chenille Bedding on the second shift at the cotton mill. She worked hard to provide for us."

Floyd described living in a rented space in an old storefront building on Highway 41 his mom had found for her and the seven children. "It wasn't much, old and dusty, but it gave us a place to sleep and to call home.

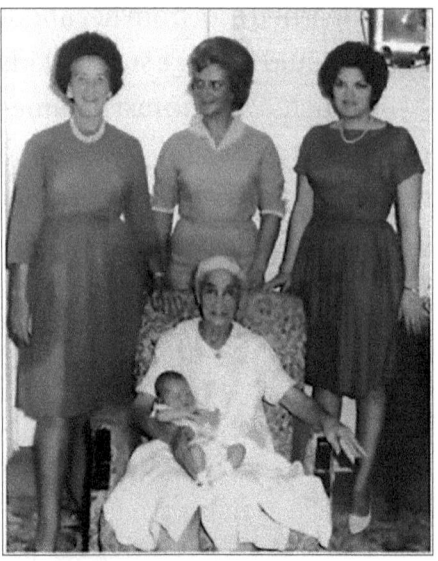

Five generations of strong women— from left: Floyd's mother, Roxie, Floyd's sister, Louise, his niece, Glenda, and Floyd's grandmother, Daisy, holding his great nephew, Robbie

"Working the second shift meant neighbors helped to keep an eye on us kids until mom got home late in the evenings. One day, I remember, I was just a little ole boy playing in the road, on Highway 41, when the Greyhound bus came roaring down the street. I guess I didn't notice it coming and the driver didn't see me until he almost ran me over. The driver had to stop the bus in the middle of the road; he jumped out to check on me and then got back in the bus and drove off.

Hard Times and Heritage 23

"I didn't think much about it. But when Mama got home from work the neighbor came running over to tell her, 'Floyd was playing in the street and stopped a Greyhound bus!'"

With a deep sigh and sunken shoulders, Floyd shook his head and said, "Mama wore my butt out."

The family's time in Calhoun provided for their needs but took a hard toll on Roxie as a single mother.

KANNAPOLIS, NORTH CAROLINA

The early 1940s were not friendly to a young single mom with seven young children. Roxie moved Floyd and his siblings to Kannapolis, North Carolina, some 322 miles away from Calhoun to be near distant family members for support and in hopes of finding a job to sustain herself and the seven children left under her care as a single woman. Floyd learned a valuable, yet hard lesson early from watching his mama: "You do what you have to do and go on."

Facing another difficult decision to make in life, Roxie loaded the car with their belongings and headed back to familiar grounds.

"I remember on that trip to Kannapolis, the mattress strapped to the back of the car and us kids in the back seat and everything we had, as little or much as it was, was packed up tight. My dog, Puggie, got to go with us.

"The car got several flats on that trip, and the last one, Mama got out, told us to stay in the car and hitchhiked, leaving us kids there alone on the side of the road. She was doing what she had to do. Finally, she came back with my uncles. They fixed the flat, and on to Kannapolis we went."

This kind of tough love left a lasting impression with Floyd.

"While many might think it was wrong, cruel, or not safe for Mama to leave us kids in the car on the side of the road, she was doing what she had to do.

"I can't tell you how many times in life I have had to use that same mindset: you do what you have to do."

During their time in Kannapolis, the family lived in a small 12 x 30-foot GI house Roxie had found. It was a 3-room house with no electricity or water. These hard times and poor conditions formed a deep character in Floyd that would sustain him for years to come. These early, tough years began a lasting work in Floyd that he often refers to as his "grit and drive."

Floyd continued onto another emotional story he shared about his first day of school in this new place called Kannapolis:

"Mama had to go off to work, and I guess she didn't know the younger classes got out an hour earlier than my older siblings. So, when my class was let out, I began walking home, not realizing I didn't know where home was. I had tried two or three different streets, and with every turn of my little feet walking, my heart was beating and my mind hoping this would be the street where home was. It was quite a while before I found my way home. It was quite scary, but I turned out okay."

As he shared the story, the emotions from deep within this man's heart begged to be released; a few tears escaped, rolling down his cheeks after recalling this traumatic experience.

It was here in Kannapolis that Floyd began to adopt the heritage of hard work. Floyd remembers the years in Kannapolis were tough, and everyone had to pitch in to help make some money for the family. He recalls, "My brother Clyde and I would sell produce, tomatoes, and potatoes to locals door to door to earn a little extra for the family. One of our neighbors who lived in the Mill Village had a little produce truck. We would pick blackberries, and he would pay us 25 cents a gallon. Do you know how long it took to pick a gallon of blackberries? And we would come in all covered up in chiggers!

Floyd with his brother Clyde

"We even picked up liquor bottles off the street and out of trash cans to turn into the local bootlegger for pennies on each bottle. He would give us a nickel for every bottle we brought to him; they had to be washed, the label cleaned off, and the screw top with it."

The days his family spent living in the Frog Holler community near Kannapolis were both challenging and rewarding. The rewards may have been small but left lasting, pleasurable impressions.

"We didn't really know that we didn't have much. Mama always seemed to make things work out. I think it was her kind of faith. I remember she picked up a corduroy jacket at the Goodwill place. It was a men's blazer jacket, really, but Mama folded up the sleeves and tacked it up for my little short arms. That jacket became my coat for many years. I remember each time I grew a little, she would untuck a little bit of sleeve to make it just long enough to cover my arms, then sew the rest back up. Over the years, you could see the lines where she tacked it at each growing spurt I had. I wore that jacket up into my early twenties, even after I was married."

As Floyd shared this story, I saw how he was amazed with all his mama could do. After years of life, now in his eighties, he could likely properly identify this story as a reflection of how poor his family was during his early childhood. That, however, was overshadowed by his deep admiration of his mama.

"When I was nine or ten years old living in Frog Holler, which is part of a nickname for a little area in Kannapolis, we would go to the YMCA. In the summers, we would go to summer camp located in Blacksburg, Virginia. They had bunk beds in the cabins for kids to sleep and places to swim, so we'd all go skinny dipping in the lakes every day. Then we would make little crafts, some kind of beaded necklace or whatever. We had projects to do every day. The summer camp lasted about two weeks and my brother Clyde and I went up there at no charge, of course, because we were part of the YMCA.

"You can imagine all these little boys running around naked and jumping in and out of the water. I remember good thoughts about those times."

Living in Frog Holler, Floyd didn't see his father often. The years and the miles from when he had last been in Atlanta left him and his dad at a great distance. Though he didn't identify the exact year, Floyd recalled a trip to Atlanta he and Clyde made to visit his dad. Floyd recounted:

"My brother Clyde and I rode a Greyhound bus from Kannapolis to Atlanta to visit our dad. I remember the long ride; it was kinda exciting and unusual at the same time. I didn't see my dad often."

Floyd said, "I didn't really know my dad, nor why he did the things he did."

He ended this story with: "On that trip to visit him, my daddy ran off to Detroit with some lady named Mammy."

As he shared this impressionable story from his youth, you could feel Floyd's puzzled, empty, and unanswered question that still echoes in his heart today.

CHAPTER 3

Out on My Own

The Hanging Dog and Frog Holler days left Floyd with some good memories, but the times were still very difficult on his mother raising all her children alone. Floyd's mother arranged for him and his brother Clyde to spend the summer with a distant relative in Atlanta. Floyd now found himself back in Atlanta at twelve years old living in Aunt Claudia's home.

In those times higher education was anything beyond the third grade. His mother, Roxie, did not have an education, and he recalls his mama telling him, "You need more schooling, and you need to stay in Atlanta to get it."

"It was hard to understand why she would have me sent off so far away. But I trusted Mama and her tough love."

Floyd, at age twelve, now faced another tough love move, one that forced him to step into adulthood and out on his own sooner than most.

It was in Atlanta, in the Adamsville area, that he and his brother joined his Aunt Claudia at her boarding house. It was located in the area of what is now I-20 and I-285.

"I came to Atlanta at age twelve to help my aunt run a boarding house. I started school in the seventh grade at

Margaret Fayne School in Adamsville, out close to the Fulton County Airport where I-20 and 285 meet on the west side. Of course, at that time, the airport had no lights on the runways, so they closed it down every day at dark.

"I remember as I was starting school, my mama sent me some money and clothes, and that's the first time I ever had underwear because in North Carolina, we didn't have nothing, nothing much really. But I thought I was something else then; I had new underwear and a new pair of blue jeans and penny loafers!

"I have some good memories of that time. I was a member of the patrol; I helped kids cross the street. We would go to the Fox Theater on Saturday and get in for, I think it was like, 10 to 25 cents, and our little girlfriends would go with us on the bus. We were twelve and thirteen years old. I really enjoyed that time in my life. But I do remember being away from home for about a year before Mama ever came down to Georgia. I was missing her. Overall, I got some good memories from that period of my life."

Floyd at age twelve "out on his own"

At the age of twelve, in a new place much larger than he had ever experienced, forced to be a man in a boy's body and with a boy's mind, Floyd quickly settled in. He earned his stay with Aunt Claudia by doing yard work, chores, stringing beans, and becoming a jack of all trades.

"Working at the boarding house, I did everything I could to help Aunt Claudia: fixing leaky faucets, cleaning rooms, helping in the kitchen, gardening, washing windows. I guess you could say I was a good all round handyman. Aunt Claudia was like a second mama to me."

He does recall making a trip by bus back to Kannapolis to visit his mother during his time in Atlanta at Aunt Claudia's:

"I grew up in a home of 'tough love.' It was instilled in me that 'you do in life what you have to do.' That was how I was able to get on a bus, alone, at thirteen years old and travel some 322 miles away to visit my mama."

Floyd recalls one of his visits back to Kannapolis when he was about fifteen or sixteen:

"My sister's husband, Arthur, had a little .22 Lever-Action Marlin gun I wished I had the money to buy. He was asking $30 for it. I didn't have quite that much, but I did have some saved-up money with me that I offered to Arthur, so he made a deal with me, and I brought that gun back on the bus to Atlanta with me. I wrapped it up in a pillowcase; of course, it came apart into two short pieces.

"Back in those days, nobody didn't think nothing about something like that. They didn't ask me what it was, and I didn't tell. After I got to the downtown Atlanta Greyhound bus station, I had to walk to Westview Drive and hitchhike the rest of the way home to Adamsville carrying that gun in a pillowcase. I still have that gun; I think the world of it because of the memories that I had with it."

Floyd's years in Atlanta seemed to provide some good turning points for his life. This is where he met his best friend, Norman Huff. Floyd affectionately recalls:

"I met Norman when we both attended Atlanta City School Margaret Fayne in junior high school. We did a lot of running around together. He was my best friend."

Floyd began the eighth grade at Southwest High School on Glenhurst Road and completed his schooling graduating in the first Senior Class of SHS in 1956.

When he was thirteen years old, Floyd remembers his mother married Carl "Connie" Irving from Kannapolis. Shortly after their marriage, they moved to Atlanta, and his mama presented the opportunity for Floyd to rejoin his family.

"She told me, I can feed you and give you a place to sleep, but you gotta buy your own shoes and clothes. Anything else you want you have to pay for."

"While that felt very tough, I knew she was teaching me responsibility."

This message of tough love was not new to him. His mother had woven this tough love philosophy and strong determination into his life in each decision she had made over the years. It only served to reinforce what he had already concluded: "Life's adversities would be my teacher."

"I learned a lot from my mama. She was tough. She could lay brick, pour concrete, cut hair. She gardened and canned for our family and sewed our clothes. Even years later, for my kids—her grandkids—she made a lot of their clothes. Mama could do anything; she was self-sufficient."

Watching his mother over the years demonstrate strong character and tough love, Floyd recalls one incident that about broke her:

"In 1958, my brother Clyde, who was the next sibling older than me, joined the Navy when he was seventeen. He was stationed in Bermuda, and Mama loved him. He was a great guy. Of course, I forgave him for kicking my butt so many times when he was young, but I guess I probably deserved it.

"Mom and Connie had gone to North Carolina to visit her kinfolks, and she didn't want me to stay in the house. I guess her tough love again. So I got me a room at a boarding house in West End. And later on that night, it was about 8 or 9:00 that I went to Adamsville to check on Mama's house because she had asked me to. I was fixing to leave when a gentleman in Navy clothes walked up to the door and wanted to know if Miss Irving was there. And, of course, I said no, that I was her son. And he said, 'Well, I've got some bad news.' He said, 'Your brother Clyde got killed in Bermuda yesterday.' I was shocked, and that news really tore me up because Clyde was the brother just older than me, and we were great friends and loved each other very much."

With the hint of a large lump in his throat, Floyd continued:

"I knew I had to call my mom and tell her what I had just been told. That was a hard thing to do. I knew she would take the news hard. You have obstacles in life that you don't think you can overcome, but with enough willpower, you got to, because there's really no one to give it up to."

HARD WORKING DAYS

Just barely fourteen years old, Floyd started his first official job as a window washer for a mere $7 a week. He worked hard after his school classes and on Saturdays.

"I was going to high school, Southwest High School, and I'd hitchhike every day to go to West End to work. I washed windows six days a week. I got $1 for each weekday and $2 for Saturday.

"Of course, I was fourteen at the time, and Mama told me that if I wanted a higher education that I had to get out and buy my books and clothes. She would feed me and give me a place to stay. But I had to go to work for anything else I wanted to buy. That was her tough love, but I think that's a lot of what made me who I am.

"I remember one week after graduating high school and barely making $50 a week, Mama told me I had to start paying room and board of $10 a week. While I thought it was kinda harsh then, I realize now her tough love taught me how to be responsible."

While in high school working as a window washer, one of Floyd's friends told him Sears was hiring a shoe salesman.

"Sears and Roebuck would hire you when you turned sixteen. So, I applied for the job. I filled out an application, talked with the manager, and walked out with a real job. That's where I learned that the harder you work, the more money you make. They sold on straight commission; men's and women's shoe sales got 6 percent, and children's was 8 percent. So I made $40-$50 a week back in those days, which was a lot of money. But I was hustling shoes on Thursday night, Friday night, and all day Saturday, and washing windows the other weekdays.

"I worked my way through high school from sixteen, seventeen, eighteen at Sears and Roebuck. I bought a car, clothes, anything I had to have or wanted to. I had the income to buy."

Floyd recalls, "Easter shoes were selling for $2.95 that year and my commission on each pair was about 6-8 percent or 23 cents per pair I sold."

Working hard and working multiple jobs was part of Floyd's ambition, part of his drive and passion. Working hard with several jobs in those high school years, he finally saved up enough to buy his first car, a 1955 Belair 22 Black and White. I paid $50 for that car, and I loved it!"

He was quite proud of that car and his ability to make owning his very own car a reality. Floyd took good care of it. But just a few weeks before prom, he wrecked it. Asking his mother if he could borrow her car to take his date to the prom, his mother asked him: "Son, where is your car?"

"Why, Mama, you know, I wrecked it."

She immediately said, "And how do I know you won't wreck my car? My answer is no."

While his mother's response may have seemed cold and hard to swallow, Floyd knew his mama was helping him learn the hard lessons of responsibility. But that didn't stop him from asking his girlfriend's dad to borrow *his* car.

"Me and my date didn't get to use the family car, but we did get to the prom in the borrowed work truck, an old jeep paint truck that my girlfriend's dad loaned me. It smelled like turpentine, but it got me and my date to the prom."

Floyd knew two things growing up: work and work. He had it instilled in him early that you do whatever it takes. That's why in the tenth grade work release program at school, he said, "I hitchhiked to work. Not having a car wasn't going to stop me from getting to work.

36 THE MAKING OF A LEGACY

"I think the hardship of finding a way and means to get to work for years before I had my first car planted in me a deep appreciation for the things I worked for and earned."

Floyd's 1955 Belair 22
Black and White

CHAPTER 4

Building a Foundation on the Working Road

Just two weeks after graduating high school, Floyd had an opportunity knock on his door to apply for a job in the construction/millwork industry. Not knowing anything about the industry didn't stop him from applying for the job. Floyd's life up until that point had prepared him to go after anything. He often said: "I have always believed I could do anything I put my mind to."

Floyd walked away from that interview with his first full-time job.

Floyd was the first male from his mother's side of the family to graduate high school. He had accomplished a milestone in his family. And now Harbor Plywood is where Floyd would begin his lifetime career in millwork.

Young Floyd Davis

HARBOR PLYWOOD—1956

Floyd quickly began to showcase his fearless nature when he entered the construction business.

"In 1956, just after graduating high school and working two jobs now, a friend of mine at Sears, Mike McGraw, gave me a heads up that Harbor Plywood was hiring a telephone salesperson, and it paid a monthly salary of $240.

"I didn't really know anything about the construction or millwork business, but I knew sales positions paid, so I went for it! I knew I could do it." Floyd continued his part-time work at Sears and Roebuck while learning a new full-time job. In the first few weeks on the job, Floyd quickly found that this new opportunity came with its challenges.

"I would go in ahead of the rest of the crew at 7:30 p.m.; everyone else got there at eight. I would go in at 7:30 and open up and put on the coffee or whatever needed to be done and start answering the phone if it rang.

"Day one of the job I got my first call. I was there early, nobody there but me. I'm in the office all by myself and the phone rings. The caller asked, 'You guys got any T-Astragals?'

"I remember the call like it was yesterday! It was Tom Elder, with Elder Building Supply, asking if we had any T-Astragals. Not having the slightest idea of what a T-Astragal was, I told him let me get a number, I'd check and buzz him right back.

"I had no idea what a T-Astragal was! I didn't tell him that, I just told him 'I don't know, but I'll find out and give you a call back.' So when Mike McGraw got there, he told me what a T-Astragal was and told me what and how it was used and gave me an education on T-Astragals! I found out that day what a T-Astragal was and *who* Tom Elder was!

"l called the customer, Tom Elder, back to let him know we had some in stock, all the while sounding like I knew what I was talking about. That was learning from somebody who had been in the business a long time! Mike taught me a lot."

Little did Floyd know how much of an impact that one phone call from Tom Elder would have on his future as he was just beginning his millwork career. Nor did he, at the time, realize how important it was that his connections in the industry were beginning to grow. The construction and millwork industry was new to Floyd, but that did not stop him from giving it his all; in fact, it fueled his drive for even more.

Floyd's early character-building years prepared him to always accept a challenge and remain willing to learn.

"Looking back, I consider the Sears and Roebuck job got me into the millwork industry. If it hadn't been for Mike McGraw, who was selling shoes there part-time, talking me into applying for the job with Harbor Plywood where he also worked, I might not be where I am today. But it was a huge learning curve for me. At nineteen years old, I took on a job without any true knowledge, skills, or experience. Harbor Plywood took a risk on me and hired me for $240 a month. That was my salary in the millwork industry back in the day, 1956, when I first got started.

"Anyway, I worked there for three years and then went to work at Zuber Lumber Company."

In the years following high school, Floyd poured into working several jobs and banking his hard-earned bucks. The extra hours, hard work, and juggling several jobs helped him purchase his first home.

"When I got the money to buy my first house in Douglasville, Georgia, I was working at Sears and Roebuck. I had graduated high school, but I wasn't making much money at my full-time job. I'd work at Sears on Thursday, Friday, and Saturday nights along with my full-time job at Harbor Plywood during the weekdays, 7:30 a.m. to 5 p.m. I was able to save up a good bit of cash. That's how I had most of the money to make the down payment on that house. But I was $400 shy.

"I had a '55 Chevrolet that was paid for, and there was a loan place up near West End, and I talked to them about borrowing the $400 for the rest of the down payment. I said I'd pay it back in six months."

Floyd wondered if he'd ever be able to make the payment. "But knowing there was a big penalty if I didn't get it paid off in time, I pinched every penny I could and finally paid the note off—on time! That's where I was working when Angela and I got married, was Harbor Plywood."

Floyd worked hard at Harbor Plywood for about three years. He considers his years at Harbor Plywood the foundation time for him in building relationships and learning the construction/millwork industry. Both of which paid off for him.

ZUBER LUMBER COMPANY—1959

Construction was a new industry and a new opportunity for Floyd. He knew he could do it. Catching on fast and doing well in sales, his confidence grew and soon another local construction company caught his interest.

"They were looking to hire someone for the 'snake pit,' their inside phone sales position, starting at $300 a month."

Lacking knowledge in millwork terminology, product details, marketing, sales, logistics, or any core knowledge required to sell industry products, Floyd jumped right into the snake pit just like he knew what he was doing!

"Zuber Lumber Company was a wholesale millwork place. They were big in building exterior windows and doors and sold moulding. They were a pretty good size outfit, and I worked in the sales office on the order desk known as the snake pit.

"They were a big distributor of Formica plastic before new countertop products were introduced. They were distributors for the state of Georgia.

"So, you got a lot of calls in what they call the snake pit. And it was a big learning curve for me because I was exposed to a lot of products that I wasn't familiar with. You had to learn and learn fast.

"As I was trying to keep sales going, I noticed we kept running out of moulding. We bought fir moulding from the West Coast in boxcar loads. It was about a six-to-eight-week delay from ordering new inventory to getting products delivered to us here on the East Coast. And I had some customers that would buy 10,000 feet at a time. We'd be out of fir moulding for three or four months at a time. So, I had an idea. I went to Miss Lockridge who was over the purchasing department, and I said, 'Can I have a PO?'

"She didn't ask for what, so I ordered $15,000 worth of moulding and casing, so we wouldn't be running out every day.

"It's a wonder they didn't fire me over that one, but Mr. Gilbert called me into his office, and he said, 'Why did you do that?' I said, 'Hell, I gotta have something to sell; we stay out of moulding and casing all the time!'"

Floyd quickly gained the confidence of his employer with that risky but successful order. It also confirmed deep within Floyd what he already knew, "You do what you have to do."

"I knew this job might be a bit of trial and error in the learning process, but I've never been afraid to try anything new," Floyd said with a grin of confidence shining on his face.

Floyd worked his new position with Zuber Lumber while continuing to work at Sears as a shoe salesman on weekends. He also took on the work of another part-time job at Wilson

Freight Lines on Saturday nights. Working seven days a week was the only work ethic he knew—nothing less.

It was during his years at Zuber Lumber Company that his wealth of knowledge in the industry grew. He also had the opportunity to gain his first purchasing and inventory flow experience. Floyd attributes the unfolding of the next season of his career to "the steep learning-curve I took on working the snake pit."

ELDER BUILDING SUPPLY—1962

Floyd's next job move landed him in retail sales and a small bump in income for his growing family—$325 a month.

Elder Building Supply was a retail job. Their retail products included different building components, trusses for roofs, and house framing kits. They sold Pittsburg Paint and paint products, brick and mortar, and sheetrock. It was also the same "Tom Elder" that called on Floyd's first job with Harbor Plywood.

"To this day I don't think I ever confessed to Tom that I didn't know what T-Astragal was when he called," Floyd said smiling. "I felt it best to keep that to myself."

It was here Floyd learned new aspects of the building industry. He was given the opportunity to be involved in every part of the company's operations.

"Elder Building Supply, which was a retail lumber business, was totally different from what I was used to. Inventory supply, warehouse management, and face-to-face customer service were all new levels of this industry for me. I found all these areas of running a business fascinating, and parts of it were second nature to me. I was eager to learn more.

"They also made trusses and prefab small houses for a contractor that was building them out around Adamsville. I stayed there over three years and got a lot of good lessons about the retail lumber business. I hadn't been in lumber; I had mainly been in millwork. At Elder Building Supply, I learned about buying two-by-fours, two-by-eights, two-by-tens or whatever in box carloads. But after I was there for about three years, I decided that I needed to move on. And I think my salary at the time was about $325 a month, which is way under what we needed. So, I left there and moved on to TP Lumber."

The three years Floyd spent at Elder Building Supply grounded him deeper into the industry. With his knowledge in this industry increasing, his relationships with contractors growing stronger daily, and his experience in this field expanding, Floyd's confidence grew.

TP LUMBER—1963

Seven years now into working in the industry, Floyd had begun to develop many friends and customers in and around the Atlanta area. As he was seeking out his next career move, he ran across an opportunity for a partnership in a lumber company.

"When I quit my job at Elder, I invested some money in TP Lumber Company, which turned out to be a farce. But anyway, I was doing outside sales for TP Lumber. As an outside salesman and doing some traveling, I was working in Chattanooga, Tennessee, and I didn't have any money to take

Building a Foundation on the Working Road

with me for anything. I remember my first call that day at this supply company. I introduced myself, and this guy talked for a minute or two. Then he decided we would go out to see if we could sell some of these panels that I was trying to sell to him to some contractors he knew in the area. But when we got in his car, he said, 'Let's stop and get a cup of coffee.' Well, I didn't have any money. I didn't have not one red cent in my pocket. That was kind of embarrassing.

"He bought my coffee, and I spent the day with him. And he did buy half a carload of that junk particle board TP Lumber had me out peddling. I think he probably done that out of just feeling sorry for me."

The TP Lumber investment and what looked like a promising partnership turned out to be a hard, hurtful lesson for Floyd. He recalls: "That business was not run well. It had low-quality products and not everyone was on the up and up. It was a fiasco. I lost $1,200 that I invested in TP."

The TP business venture was not an easy story for Floyd to recall.

"The hardest part of that for me was, I had rented out the little house on Lake Monroe Drive in Douglasville, and Angela and I were living in a little apartment over off Campbellton Road in Ben Hill. We had three kids, and she was pregnant with the fourth. Losing that money hurt not just me but my family!"

The road of business ventures, new investments, and reaching for greater opportunity sometimes has major bumps, life lessons, and what many would call failures. What could have been a major setback for Floyd—this venture, this investment, this opportunity gone bad—he took as, "It's something you have to overcome—adversity—no matter what."

One story he recalls from his time at TP Lumber while out making sales calls involves an encounter with two hitchhikers.

"I remember traveling back from Chattanooga one evening close to dusk. I saw these two colored boys, hitchhikers, on the highway. I didn't think it was safe for them at dusk hitching a ride, so I stopped. Turned out they were about seventeen, eighteen years old and had left, run away from home. Well, I showed up at the apartment with them, and Angela and I took them in for about two or three weeks. They worked at a local car wash to get up enough money to get a bus ticket back home. We had written to their mother to let her know what was going on and that they would be coming home soon. She was very thankful."

GEORGIA FLUSH DOORS—1964

While the TP Lumber fiasco made it seem like he was taking a step backward, Floyd stepped up his game and began looking for an inside sales position in the area with great potential. "After TP Lumber, I went to Georgia Flush Door. I was looking for inside sales, when I went to apply for the job at Georgia Flush. I got it."

Things were looking up again for Floyd. Although it was a small millwork distributor mainly focused on interior and exterior doors, Floyd saw great potential in the business.

"I went to work there in January. Their sales that month were something like $40,000. Well, I had been used to working for Zuber Lumber Company whose sales were more like $700,000 to $800,000 a month.

"They didn't deliver, they didn't have salespeople. So, I was worried. I got a wife and four kids at home depending on this place to keep my family up. And I thought, *Well, we need to add some products here and there, and I know this place could do a lot more if he made deliveries.* They had good quality products, but it all had to be picked up, and he was just in the door business and wasn't in any of the other millwork items.

"I had an idea!

"Walt liked to drink a beer every day after work. So, we went down to the little pub there on McDonough Street, and we're sitting there talking, and I said, 'You know, Walt, I think that we could add some lines here and really increase your business.'

"He thought about it for a minute and then said, 'I tell you what to do— whatever you want to do, figure it up, what it costs, and if I can afford it, we'll try.'"

Little did Floyd realize he had just been handed a lifetime opportunity. He was given the go-ahead to build a business with someone else's money.

"I started adding on lines like bifold doors, stair parts, and linear moulding instead of just seven foot for the door unit. That business grew until I left it in 1975. It grew from $40,000 a month to over $800,000 in sales each month.

"He made a lot of money with all the changes and additions. He didn't ever pay me to run the place, but I ended up more or less doing just that. That's where I got my experience with all the West Coast suppliers at that time because most of your moulding and casing came from the West Coast. I made a lot of trips to the West Coast. I got to travel, mainly just to buy and check out new products and buy fir doors from Jeld Wen, and a lot of other folks. It was such a good experience for me to do that.

"We grew the business and when I left in 1975, they were doing about $800,000 a month instead of $40,000. I made a lot of money and the biggest bonus I ever got, he paid me 1 percent of the profit."

Floyd's gamble to take a hefty risk and join up with another smaller company—starting all over—paid off big. Floyd's grit and drive, passion, and desire for greater things pushed him right into one of his best career moves. Not only did he receive 1 percent commission on company profits, but he also began to extend his knowledge of the millwork industry, create an extensive network of customers nationwide, and grow the company netting over $8 million annually. And, his relationship with the West Coast Jeld Wen Company would be yet another future connection.

"At Georgia Flush Doors, I more or less ran the company; everything, including all purchases. Angela and I went to all the conventions, one in New York, San Francisco, Houston, the Cayman Islands. A poor old country boy like me is not used to all that fancy traveling, but we enjoyed it. We also got to buy some new clothes."

During his time at Georgia Flush Doors, Walt and Howard Knapp allowed Floyd the freedom to expand the business to include new services and products, increasing the company's bottom-line profits. Floyd introduced delivery services that cost little in overhead and brought in remarkable profit. He expanded the warehouse, allowing for larger inventory and sales.

Floyd treated the business just as if it were his own: "When I left in 1975, I had been instrumental in growing this small market company into a million-dollar nationwide supplier."

Floyd in his early business years

During the time Floyd worked at Georgia Flush, there were social tensions in the area. Dr. Martin Luther King, Jr.'s funeral was held, labor unions were seeking a foothold in the South, and there was social unrest in opposition to the draft and the United States' involvement in the Vietnam War. Each of these social pressures affected work environments across the South. Floyd recalls an incident he not only witnessed but was intimately involved in, one that threatened him and took the life of a friend and coworker.

"Georgia Flush Door, it was over on Capitol Avenue and University, which was on the pretty bad side of town. We even had an employee sitting in his car that they robbed and carried over to Campbellton Road and tied him to a tree. Bob Gore was his name.

"Mr. Knapp had fired two of the employees there who were of color. And they had been calling in, threatening, so Walt was downtown getting a restraining order, so they wouldn't come to the office, but he didn't get it in time. About 3:30 or 4:00 in the afternoon, they showed up at Georgia Flush Door. There's two of them in the car, and it was Powell Steel, another inside salesman and myself in the office. When you come in the front door, there's a plexiglass window on the right, and I was around that corner sitting with my back to the window. One of the guys came in, and I was watching him. He started putting his hand in his pocket. It all happened so fast, but I remember Powell thought he was probably gonna pull out a gun or a knife, so Powell shot him in the leg.

"When the guy that was riding with him, Freddy Gude, heard the shot from the car out there, he came in with the deer rifle, came through the door, and shot through the plexiglass and hit Powell Steel right in the neck. And he killed him.

"When he shot him, he came on around the corner, and I thought, *He's gonna shoot me next,* but he seen that he killed Powell. And he ran, left. Of course, the police caught him I think the next day. But what had led up to it was some of the Teamsters who were out trying to organize labor unions.

"That was a tragedy and very traumatic! It's not a pleasant memory. I do know, however, the good Lord was looking out after me in that one."

In the '70s, there was a big push for organized labor unions in the South. Georgia Flush Door was approached by the organizers of these unions and found themselves facing the possibility of becoming unionized.

"I remember Walt hired a lawyer in Atlanta. He advised Walt to write a letter to the union stating how good they were to their employees, what benefits they offered, and how they planned to continue to treat their employees well. While that all sounded nice, we were up against a crunch. There was a planned 'vote' the upcoming Tuesday, and only employees that were on payroll by Thursday would be allowed to vote. So, what we did was, I pooled all our employees together and hired about ten more before the deadline. One of our employees was a part-time salesperson, and when the union organizers interviewed all the employees, they didn't question or object to the part-time employee participating in the vote. As it turns out, that part-time employee was the one vote that beat out the union organization at our business."

Floyd had a good working relationship with Walt and Howard Knapp as he approached a decision to leave Georgia Flush Doors. Floyd's contributions to the company helped to expand the business, increase the company's bottom line, turn larger warehouse inventory into sales, and bring in remarkable profits. In 1974, just before leaving, Floyd earned a $27,000 bonus from Georgia Flush Doors. He used this to pay off debt, place a down payment on a $29,000 house in Douglasville, and used some of the cash to help start his next business venture.

While going to church regularly was not part of Floyd's family habits most of his life, he does have a keen recall of certain times he knew the good Lord had been watching out for him. "The Greyhound bus almost ran me over in my early years when we lived in Calhoun, Georgia. The times

Mama put me on the bus at twelve years old to travel alone, the Powell Steel shooting while I was here at Georgia Flush Doors, and now this large bonus, along with the opportunity to learn all I did here, let me know Someone bigger than me was watching out for me."

CHAPTER 5

True Grit and Drive

In 1975, Floyd stepped out on his own and started Floyd Davis Sales (FDS). Using a good portion of the profit bonus he had received working at Georgia Flush Doors, he set out to start his own business. From his first job with Harbor Plywood in 1956, he had developed a respectable reputation, and now, as an independent manufacturing representative, he was able to use his cross-country network of relationships in the industry to begin generating sales in his own business venture.

Floyd recalls: "It took me right at $12,000 to get started as an independent rep, and I traveled over 127,000 miles in my first year.

"When I had quit my job at Georgia Flush Door, I went out as a manufacturer's rep, and I stayed on the road a lot. The first year, I drove 127,000 miles calling on customers from Virginia to Alabama, Georgia, Florida, North Carolina, and South Carolina. So, I stayed on the road all the time. After about two years of that, Angela told me that I needed to start staying home more, or she was going to be going out the door!"

Building a strong customer base would be crucial for launching a successful new business, but the long days of travel that kept him away from home were hard. Floyd was the sole sales force from the start, and after nearly two years on the road, it began to take a toll on his family.

"In 1977, after Angela gave me that talk, I started looking for the next opportunity to pull me in off the road. I was traveling in North Carolina near Charlotte, and I had seen on the side of the expressway a handmade road sign: 'Damaged Doors.' *Well*, I thought to myself, *I have plenty of damaged doors*, and I knew where I could get a lot more damaged doors, so I pulled off the exit. It was late one evening when I found the place and the fellow was saying he bought seconds from a mill, south down towards Savannah, and he didn't pay but one dollar a piece for them. He was making dog houses and utility storage with them and selling them. So that gave me an idea.

Original tax and expense journals for 1976-1977

"If he could do that and make money, I thought I could get a little building and sell the damaged doors out of it and show people what they could do with those doors. I knew I could sell them and make some money.

"I got to looking around and found a building in Douglasville. It was about three thousand square feet and had been a tire recapping place. Black soot and rubber were everywhere in that building. I figured it would be a good place, so I started cleaning it up, and in 1977, I started Building Material Liquidation.

"I remember my daughter, Shelly, and her little boyfriend was supposed to be helping me sweep and clean the place, and he had my 1953 Chevrolet pickup truck. Now, instead of working and sweeping the floor, he went to pick Shelly up at high school in my truck. On the way back, they wrecked the truck—hit a tree. I don't know what they was doing to take their mind off the road. But anyway, they totaled my only truck—my prized 1953 Chevy! In the millwork business, everybody knows you gotta have a truck! Now I didn't, but it didn't stop me."

With the three thousand square-foot building in Douglasville now rented and a supply of inventory on the way, it was time to open the doors to his own business.

"I had ordered a whole eighty-foot boxcar load of seconds from Temple Products. Temple Products was a company I had repped for and sold their doors all over the Southeast. So, I decided that I'll try the salvage business for a while. I rented that place in Douglasville and had the kids up there helping me, Darcy and Shelly.

"Later, I rented another place across the street from Wickes Lumber up on Highway 78, and Shelly would cry when I would try to make her work; Darcy would too. They got some good stories to tell about that. But that was the beginning of Building

Materials Liquidation (BML) and FDS. That was in 1977. We grew that place in five years into about a $500,000-a-year business. We were chasing the apartment business all over Atlanta. So, we had bought a used old machine, which was a piece of junk, but I could build pre-hung exterior doors that would route for the hinges and bore for the locks. At that time, the local market was using and selling split jamb doors. I knew we could build and sell a better product using the one-piece flat jamb with the one-piece door stop. So, I had an idea!

"We would introduce the flat jamb door into the local market! In my travels as a rep, I knew the flat jamb doors were used on the West Coast, and I knew I could modify and make our own version. So we did.

"We began selling them to the apartment contractors. These doors were easier to install and were cheap enough that they would use this one-piece flat jamb with the case and apply one side on the other. That was the beginning of Building Material Liquidation and Floyd Davis Sales."

Chasing the apartment business in the Atlanta area with a small start-up business meant Floyd would need competitive strategies. Purchasing the door machine to craft flat jamb doors and sell them was a key move for FDS and BML. He soon added another service by delivering doors directly to contractors at their job sites.

"Back in those days, they always used a solid core flush door on the front entrance, a double bore door. So, we'd have to tote them up to the stairs, starting with the third floor first. A solid core exterior door weighed about one hundred pounds! I think I weighed 160 pounds at the time. We'd have to tote them doors up three and four flights of stairs. The first flight wasn't all that bad, but the second and third floors got a little tougher! As tough as the delivery service was, it turned out to be a good thing for us getting started."

Factory closeout signage and pricing, mimicking McDonald's color scheme marketing

Floyd attributes much of the success of FDS and BML to their supply to the apartment construction booming in the Atlanta area. He began to search for bulk buys of materials and products for apartments. He supplied aluminum windows, door stops, medicine cabinets, and door hardware. He would find a manufacturer to wheel and deal a good bulk buy from and then resell to the contractor any items needed to complete an apartment build.

Floyd's knowledge of turning salvage into cash dollars was incredible. In fact, it could be described as a gift.

He had a knack for spotting a bargain buy and turning it around into dollars.

"I recall when I ran across some cedar bevel siding. The company had discarded them because they had knots in them. Well, what I saw was opportunity for a bargain and cash dollars. I was purchasing one thousand-feet board for $25 and reselling them for $125 to the contractor. We had placed an ad in the *Atlanta Journal,* and our prices were cheaper for them than buying new product. They would install the knotted bevel siding, and anywhere they found a knot, sand it down and fill in with compound. That prevented leaks and made the knotted bevel siding as good as new.

"We were selling this out of the Highway 78 location in Douglasville. I rented a flashing sign and put it out by the road. That drew in customers and was a great marketing move. But it also got the sales rep's attention. When he came in and found out what was going on, he got with his boss, and they raised my purchase price. So that kinda killed that deal, but it was a good ride for a while, and we made money from it.

"I have always had this ability to take something old, worn, broken, or thrown aside and find another purpose for it. I remember we had some 2-foot, 3-foot, and 4-foot Honduras pine interior window casing that I was able to show the contractors how to use as casing on their aluminum window installs. It turned out to be cost savings for them and helped turn an old stack of interior trim seconds into useful product and cash dollars for the salvage business."

His knowledge of the millwork industry, his connections, and his grit and drive were a unique combination. Each position Floyd had in the last twenty years had prepared him for his future.

"I had repped for Georgia Flush Door, so I had contacts to buy doors, trim, split jambs, moulding, casing, and anything an apartment job needed, because I had been in that business. While a rep for Georgia Flush Door, I knew a lot about hanging doors, and I made several trips and met some of the owners of these businesses—Jeld Wen, for instance."

Floyd recalls a story where he helped solve a huge dilemma, and yet again, little did Floyd know what an impact this would have in his future business ventures.

"Jeld Wen had a problem with selling white pine six-panel doors in Atlanta years before, and I made the trip to the West Coast, and I told him I thought we could really do a good job with those doors. So, they let me have the line here on the East Coast, and the first year at Georgia Flush, we sold twenty-four carloads of interior white pine six-panel doors instead of the fir; you couldn't get fir at the time.

"I was thankful I had the foresight to switch to white pine. And that was while I worked for Georgia Flush Door.

"Because of my relationship with the Jeld Wen people, as I was first going into operation in Douglasville, they furnished me with moulded six-panel doors that nobody else in Atlanta could get. The market here was only using Flush, Luan, and lower-market doors. The moulded six-panel pine doors helped set Floyd Davis Sales and Building Material Liquidation apart from our competitors as we were chasing the apartment business.

"They, Jeld Wen, remembered how I had helped them years earlier and, in turn, helped me out, and that's great. That's the way it should be. It was amazing. Our sales went out the roof!"

Those early days of building a business while on the road as an independent rep were hard on Floyd and his family. And the sales from the road were not generating the income needed to sustain his family of four kids and his wife. Floyd knew he had to do something because the weight of not making enough for the family was heavy, and traveling was challenging.

"When Angela told me how she hated me being on the road and wanted me to find something else, exactly what that would be, I didn't know.

"Looking back, that first year as a rep, I drove 127,000 miles, and I was doing everything I could to make it. We would even have to meet up somewhere on the road for our family vacations.

"I remember, though, how things seemed to begin to change."

"Angela and I were on our way home from a short weekend trip in Gatlinburg, and I had gotten her to promise to give me six months to make it happen, and it looked like it wasn't going to happen. So, I told her, 'Monday morning, I'll go out looking for another job.'

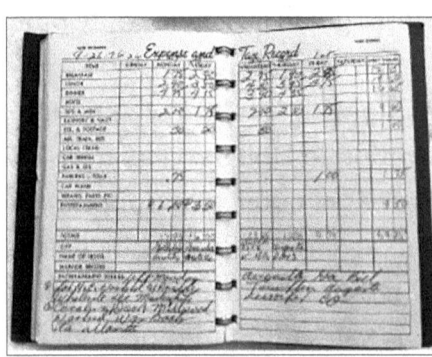

Floyd's travel journal and expense records from 1976

"Neither one of us wanted to face this devastating decision, but I knew I had to

True Grit and Drive 61

Floyd and Angela enjoying their motorcycle rides

do whatever it would take for my family, and after all, I had promised Angela.

"As an independent manufacturer's rep, you had to sell it and had to produce it. So usually, from the time you got the order until you got your commission check was two to three months. I had some stuff sold, but at the end of six months, I had run out of money. So, I told Angela that we would drive to Gatlinburg. We took the motorcycle to Gatlinburg and when we come back, I would get a job because most everyone knew me in Atlanta from the job I had done at Georgia Flush Door.

"That evening, we got home only to find a miracle in the mailbox—a $3,000 check on a commission sale from a vendor who had defaulted on payment. You should have seen the entire family jumping for joy and shouting with excitement!

"I had a commission check for $3,000, and Darcy and the kids and Angela still remember me whooping and hollering and carrying on about getting that commission check! That was the difference in me going and doing what I've wanted to do my whole life, and it turned out good. That $3,000 check went a long way. It helped to keep me in business, my own business!"

Floyd holds to the belief that major things began to change after he left his job in January of 1975 and went out on his own. While leaving the security of a steady job seemed shaky, Floyd knew he was cut out for more. His determination to take a risk paid off.

"That check was what I used to keep Floyd Davis Sales and Building Material Liquidation going. The good Lord was looking after me back then!

"That's what started everything; me quitting my job in '75 and at the end of '77."

Those early years of starting a business required all hands on deck. The girls were helping run the salvage store, Floyd was prepping damaged doors for resale after long days on the road, and Angela held her share, too.

"Angela had gone to work and had volunteered with the school to help them take inventory and was working at the shop helping to screw on hinges at night. We were working all the time. Her job started as one day a week, then they worked her two days a week. Then it got to be three, four, and five. So, she couldn't do it all, and finally quit her job. She really liked her job, but she says she liked me better."

Floyd recalls: "She was my office help. She did the paperwork. Typing, sending out letters, dealing with people, and answering the phones and advertising and stuff.

Angela working phones, payroll, and customer service

"At that time, we used pagers; it was before cell phones. If you had a cell phone, it weighed about 25 pounds; it cost $1,000 a month to make three phone calls! They were very expensive, and I remember a lot of times, I don't know how many times, I would leave my little black phone book with all my customers' information at a payphone and drive fifty miles and happen to remember it, then go back to get it!

"We were stretching it to the limit. All those 127,000 miles on the road paid off."

Floyd's BML venture began with $700 of damaged exterior fir and salvaged doors he made available to the public at discounted pricing. He also began the delivery service of doors to builders in the Atlanta area. These two simple concepts took off with great results. The profits began to roll in and monthly sales were up over half a million dollars for his new business.

"I remember when we were getting Building Material Liquidation started. It opened up with about, I think, $700 worth of damaged doors. I was a manufacturer's rep for Temple Products in Temple, Texas. They made panels, bifold, six-panel doors, six-panel exterior doors, and Masonite doors.

"I was out there for a sales meeting and walking through the warehouse, and I saw they had a stack of stuff that they had made wrong, or were damaged, or something happened to it. So, I talked him into letting me buy that from him. But I didn't know it was a boxcar load worth of goods. So, in about a month, a boxcar showed up in Douglasville. I had him put it on the team track for us to unload.

"When the doors got here, I had no truck, no forklift. I had to scratch around and come up with money to borrow an old truck from a guy in the dynamite business; he would dynamite the bottom of wells. I rented his truck, and we would drive the forklift up Highway 78, work every night to about 12 or 1:00 in the morning, unloading that 80-foot boxcar. It took several weeks to get the goods unloaded. We only had one forklift. So, we would drive the forklift down Highway 78 to the team track to unload the doors off the boxcar onto the trailer, then drive the forklift back down the highway to the shop to unload the inventory off the trailer onto the racking. We did this each night for hours at a time until that box car finally was unloaded. This was good ole fashion manual labor, but it was a good buy because there was a lot of money I made, repairing stuff, putting bifold doors together, buying hardware for simple repairs, and that kind of thing. It was selling like hotcakes.

"We'd run it in the *Atlanta Journal* newspaper. We were selling a bifold door that would normally sell for $40 to $50; we were selling them for $15 with the hardware. My costs in each unit, I wouldn't have that much in. But I made a little bit of money, which I needed to make.

"I was still traveling around the country, not as much as I was before I started that place, but I'd travel on the road and come in on Friday, and whatever needed to be built, I'd stay up Friday nights and build it. And then we'd be open on Saturday. But the little business grew.

"Fridays, when I got in off the road, I would check and see what they had on order to be picked up the next day, and I would work in the shop until 12 or 1:00 getting stuff ready for customers to pick up the next morning on Saturday. It was long days, hard work. But we enjoyed building a business that we could say 'look what we done.' It was kinda tough back in them days, but paid off to be rewarding."

COMPETING WITH THE BIG BOYS

With BML now established and bringing in profit, Floyd had another creative marketing idea and business venture in mind to compete with the big boys.

"There was Wickes Lumber Company on Highway 78 in Douglasville, not far from the Building Material Liquidation store—now Wickes. Because of their name, and they were a big retail business that drew a lot of traffic, I thought some of that traffic I could pull in business from. There was a building that came up for sale across the street from Wickes Lumber Company. So, I rented another building right across the street from Wickes to sell more salvage out of!

"We set up a flashing sign on our side of the road with sales prices, right across from Wickes entrance, and drew customers in that small salvage place. The store across from

Wickes, we sold second-hand paneling, moulding; anything I could find at a deal, I'd buy it, and we'd sell it.

"People were coming to Wickes, they were building supply people; they were retail building supply operations. They sold lumber, windows, doors, and millwork. So being across the street from their entrance, I thought that'd be a heck of a location; and the flashing sign might have had a small part," Floyd offered with a grin as he continued to share.

"The little building I rented was probably 2,000 square feet, a small operation. I didn't have anybody else to run it. So, the girls, Shelly and Darcy, were fifteen and sixteen when I introduced them into the business at a young age. They were still in high school. They ran the small second-hand store basically by themselves.

"After a few years, I sold it to my brother Mack. He had been working for me and had come down from Detroit to deliver stuff down at Building Material Liquidation. Mack operated it for several years after.

"Shelly always said, 'If I'd known then what I know now, I would have bought that from you!'" Floyd recalls.

Floyd with his brother Mack

EXPANDING BML

As the door and window salvage business began to take off, Floyd was thinking ahead and willing to move forward with new risks.

"I needed more room," Floyd said. "There was a house that had burned behind the tire recap place. I had purchased the tire recapping place after being there a year. He sold it to me for $30,000, and, of course, I had to scout around, get up the money somewhere. But anyway, we got money to buy the land. And I was growing—the business was growing.

"So, I borrowed the money, enough money to buy the land with a burned house on it behind BML and proceeded to try to get enough assets up to build a building. This was in the late '70s early '80s, and it was a recession time when the economy was down in the pits.

"I decided I needed to put up a 20,000-square-foot metal building for more room to grow the business. Melvin Prichett sold me the building. He was a commercial building contractor down in Lithia Springs. He had somebody who ordered a 20,000-square-foot building and didn't take it, and he was in a tight spot for money. So, he sold me that building for $20,000, which is $1 a square foot for a metal building, which is unheard of. But he needed the money, and I needed the building, and so we worked a deal out."

The ability and timing to run across "deals" seemed to be part of Floyd's story. With each additional business venture, things seemed to fall into place for Floyd.

"I never had any experience putting up metal buildings. But it's my nature 'If you can't figure it out, you find another way or you try to do it yourself,' so that's what we done.

"I proceeded then to start grading off down there, bulldozing down the burned house remains and filling in a little pond to put up my metal building on, just like I knew what I was doing! I started hauling in dirt to fill in low spots. I put the forms up for the concrete, and I poured the slab.

"I proceeded to try to figure out how to put up a building. I had Brian Lacey who had helped me in Wedowee. So, Brian helped me to lay the building out. I got the bolt layout and procedure to drill holes and fix the layout for the beams. That building was 100 feet wide and 200 feet long. It was huge!

"After we got the pad poured and the bolts set, we started hanging the steel beams. I didn't have a machine that would pick up a beam that was 50 feet long, and so I borrowed a crane from across the railroad tracks from Young Asphalt Company. You needed a crane to pick up the steel beams that sat on top.... It leaked hydraulic fluid, and about the time you pick the long beam up and start to set it down, it would lose pressure and you couldn't stop it. You had to hit the right spot with it, but after several tries, we got fairly decent at setting the beams and got that building up.

"This old worn-out lift would sputter and about the time we would get a beam strapped, the old crane wouldn't hold pressure, and it would start back down. When it started back down, you had to let it hit the ground and start all over again. It took us many a try, but we got pretty good at hitting it in the right place. I bet we used 300 gallons of hydraulic fluid just squirting out of that old machine alone. But we finally got it up. We learned a lot on that project. I got pictures of us putting the building up.

"I didn't have the money at the time to insulate the building. So, we put it up with the metal on the framing without the insulation."

The fact Floyd did not have experience putting up a metal-framed building didn't stop him. In his mind, *There's nothing I can't do or at least try; you can always figure out a way.* That building served its purpose many years over and still houses BML operations to this day.

"That's when I also bought a door machine. In 1987, I had a house down in Gulfport, Mississippi, that me and Angela really loved to go to. I had it for about three years, and I needed some money to get the high production door machine because at that time, we were after the apartment business, and there was no way I could produce enough to do apartments with the equipment I had there.

"I sold that little place in Biloxi, Mississippi, that we'd bought and really enjoyed using as a vacation place, but I needed a door machine, so I sold it and bought a $50,000 door machine. I still miss that little place in Biloxi, Mississippi, and Angela does too. That was a big sacrifice for us both! But it has paid off."

Stepping out on his own in 1975 was a huge risk. Starting BML and the salvage business was an even greater risk. But risks didn't faze Floyd. In fact, he seemed to thrive on them. As he began to wrap up this session of storytelling, you could

THE MAKING OF A LEGACY

hear the humble, eighty-five-year-old speak most proudly of his risky accomplishments.

"I opened up Douglasville in 1977. We sold doors and windows; that was another reason I sold the house in Biloxi, Mississippi, was to get another building in Douglasville and expand our operations.

"Chasing the apartment business in Atlanta, I needed the door machine, and why I sold the house in Mississippi was to buy the $50,000 machine. We could run four hundred interior units a day there, and our sales went to half a million a month from that salvage business we opened in '77.

"We were doing about half a million dollars a month furnishing doors, trim, locks, and medicine cabinets—anything that went on the multifamily apartment business in Atlanta."

Little did Floyd know that business would continue to grow for the next several decades.

Banner with Floyd's quote still hanging today in BML warehouse

CHAPTER 6

Satellite Businesses

The success of FDS and BML made room for more creative business opportunities over the next several decades. Soon BML became a hub for several other sales outlets Floyd set up. Not only was the salvage business growing, but other building supply opportunities caught his attention.

"We had about six different little satellite businesses for what I call the junk business or salvage operation. But we had a small satellite place in Woodstock selling doors and trim. I started a sheetrock business in the Douglasville location and then we moved the sheetrock business up to Woodstock and purchased a thirty-something-thousand boom truck that we could offload by putting the sheetrock panels through the window on the second floor. Made the delivery service much easier and more profit because deliveries didn't take as long to offload. Saved manpower and labor and made more time for more deliveries when the contractors needed it for their install schedule. You didn't get the business if you couldn't deliver when the contractor needed the product.

The apartment building business was taking off in that area, and so the windows and doors sales, along with the sheetrock business, really thrived up there.

"With me knowing the millwork resale of salvaged items and getting the contractors buy for their projects, this little business grew pretty fast. So, I opened a few more little satellites of salvage sales and millwork businesses; I had one in Nashville, Tennessee, one in Cartersville, Georgia, one in Norcross, Georgia, and Woodstock, Georgia, and I had a retail place in Knoxville, Tennessee, along with Knoxville Door and Millwork, my big operation in Knoxville.

"I also had a larger operation in Blacksburg, Virginia. It was a two-step operation like Knoxville Door and Millwork. A two-step operation would sell to a dealer, and the dealer would sell to the contractor. But we covered more toward the eastern part of the US with that operation."

The year 1975 was a pivotal year for Floyd. That was the year he stepped out on his own to begin what he had no idea would be a lifelong journey of business ventures. Each venture held its own risk factors, but risks did not scare Floyd. He believed he could succeed at whatever he put his mind to.

Over the next few years, Floyd chased the opportunities along with their risks. Some ventures paid off, while others he packed up and closed down.

"I always needed a challenge. And I seem to have the ability to look into situations to see if I can make it turn into money."

SHEETROCK BUSINESS

"Just like how the sheetrock business got started, years later. When my birth dad, Joe, was in the hospital in Atlanta with cancer of the liver, there was another gentleman in the room with him, Harold Pruitt, and in walks a guy I had met twenty years ago when he was driving a truck.

"We just got to talking and he said that he had gotten into the sheetrock business and was really making good money. That flared my interest. So, I asked him, 'What all do I need to get into the sheetrock business?' He said, 'Well, you need a warehouse and you need a forklift. And you need a jack truck where you can go straight up with the load of sheetrock, so you can put it into the second-floor window.'

"All that intrigued me, and I got to do a little research and decided that's what I needed to do, is to get into the sheetrock business. I knew a bunch of builders around Douglasville I thought I could sell to. So, I ordered a trainload of sheetrock and half a trainload of sheetrock mud, tape, and everything it took to get in the business. I built a shed right behind Millworks in Douglasville; in fact, the slab is still there.

"Our first order I got was from Bud Lee. He was building some houses down in Lithia Springs. I talked with Bud and told him, 'I sure would like to have your sheetrock business.' So he gave me two houses to pull a sheetrock order for. Me and Brian, who was working for me, had a plan. I was gonna get in the sheetrock business and do it after five every day because we had to be there running the store until five. Everything has a learning curve!

"We put one house order of sheetrock on the truck, and I looked at it, and I said, 'Man, that ain't much sheetrock;

let's just take both houses since they're side by side.' What a mistake that was!

"We got down to the job and got it unstrapped, backed up to the door, pulled off two pieces of sheet rock, and we had to step up about a 12-inch step.

"We did get those pieces in the house. Then we proceeded to unload the rest of it, and of course, it had to be put in different rooms. But we started about 6:00 in the evening and got through about 2:00 in the morning. Our knuckles were skinned up and bleeding; I was so sore I couldn't hardly wiggle!

But we got Bud's sheetrock business, and I thought at that time, *This is the last sheetrock I'm gonna tote*, but as it turns out, I kept doing it and got tougher where we could unload a truck that took us five to six hours in about an hour. So that was a learning curve for me."

The sheetrock business was birthed in one of Floyd's "I got an idea" moments. He took the challenge of securing a warehouse, getting in the inventory, and buying a boom truck, and started a sheetrock business and ran with it. As it turned out, it was a profit-making business for him for several years.

"We kept it going for probably three, four, or five years, but it grew, and I bought a truck that you didn't have to jack up and walk a two-by-ten into the house. I remember one big house down off Highway 166 that we got a big order of sheetrock for and went down there and scoped it out. I backed up to the second-floor window to get it upstairs. It was in November, so it was pretty chilly.

"When you're toting sheetrock, you usually burn enough energy that you would sweat profusely. But we didn't that night, and we had the truck backed up, and we were starting to take it in through the window, and it was a little windy, which we didn't know about, and I thought it was gonna blow us off the two-by-ten walking over to put it through the window. We worked 'til about 1:00 at night. We had two trucks down there to unload. It was a pretty good-sized house. And that was when I decided if I was gonna stay in the sheetrock business, I needed to buy a boom truck which puts it right up into the window, and you pull it right off.

"I did buy one and continued to grow the sheetrock business for a while and got good experience in the sheetrock business; plus, all that manual labor probably made me live a little longer."

In all his ventures, Floyd has never been afraid of hard work or failed to put in more than his share of the required labor. The sheetrock business was no different.

"I had an old friend named Bruce Armor. Bruce worked for the VisaDoor Company. They made door lights that you inserted into flush doors, either decorative lights or plain glass. That was before everything was insulated glass. Bruce worked for VisaDoor, and I bought from him when I sold those products at Georgia Flush Door. So, when I left Georgia Flush in 1975, and went out on my own as a manufacturer's rep, I would run into him occasionally.

"I had ran into him one day at a convention in Arizona. I was telling him I was gonna start a salvage business in Douglasville and how I had ordered a boxcar load of seconds and damaged doors from Temple Products, who was a company I repped for. They had sent the doors to the team track in

Douglasville. At the time, I didn't have a truck, forklift, or anything to unload them. Well, Bruce had come by the shop, and they told him I was up there unloading the boxcar. Bruce said, 'What are you doing?' and he said, 'You're crazy as hell. I don't want any part of this.'

"It was in the middle of July and sweat was running off of me as he watched me unload the boxcar load of doors.

"But four to five years later, he and I got together on a sheetrock business. I'd started the sheetrock business in Douglasville, and Bruce thought it would go well in the Woodstock area, and I did too. So I expanded the sheetrock business into Woodstock. We rented a building up there next to Woodstock Door and Trim, another one of them satellite businesses I started. And I expanded the sheetrock business. Bruce ran that part.

"There was a lot more construction going on in Woodstock than there was in Douglasville. So, I moved the operation to Woodstock. I thought that'd be the thing to do.

"That sheetrock venture, it turned out, we were very successful in that operation. We operated it for three or four years, and then Bruce wanted to buy me out, and he did. It was an experience, and that's a true story. I can't make up these things!"

Floyd's satellite business ventures were off to a great start. The Salvage Door business took off, and soon he found himself with several satellite stores from Georgia to Tennessee to Virginia.

SAWMILL BUSINESS, PRODUCTION, FAMILY OPPORTUNITIES, AND CONSTRUCTION

Throughout his years of business ventures, Floyd has always looked for opportunity. He ventured into the sawmill business in 1993 and had an operation in Wedowee, Alabama. He built a fully equipped operation complete with dry kilns, air-dry sheds, and sawmill machinery. The kilns could dry over one thousand board feet of lumber. The lumber he harvested was milled into split jambs, trusses, and other building components.

The BML location in Douglasville also became home to a high-production facility for doors. Floyd's business ventures in millwork were quickly moving him into the manufacturing and production fields.

In 1993, he repurposed some inventory from a business he sold to start a salvage business closer to home in Wedowee.

"When I sold the big business in Knoxville, we had several trailer loads of doors, damaged doors, moulding, windows, just an assortment of millwork. So, I built a building in Heflin, and since it didn't cost anything, I thought we would put another Building Material Liquidation place there, which we did. That was in 1993. And so it's been here. It's still in operation. Jeff is still working here. Darcy runs this, Shelly runs the motel, and Tonya is up in Douglasville with the Building Material Liquidation running it.

"Jeff Smith was a young man that I first met while he was working at Georgia Flush Door after I left there. They hired him to work in a shop. That was in probably '77 that he went to work at Georgia Flush Door. I needed to take Douglasville and make it more high-production millwork because we were chasing apartment jobs in Atlanta. And he had been working for someone like Georgia Flush Door for a long time; he had experience in the door business. So, he came to work for me in 1984 in Douglasville to increase production to help us go after the apartment business.

"And then when I bought Knoxville Millwork, I needed him in Knoxville because he was experienced in high production door and door machinery. He worked with me up there until I sold the business, and then he moved back to Alabama, and he still works for me now and helps run the millwork place here in Heflin."

Floyd has been most generous to his family and friends who have supported him over the years, contributing to the hard work and success of his many business ventures. His small business ventures have included a lamp business, a bonding agency, a wedding venue, rental properties of homes and townhomes, a granite business, and a motel and campgrounds business, to name just a few.

Lake Wedowee Hotel, still open for business

"My friend Jerry Spooner introduced me to a guy in the granite business, and he got to telling me how much money you can make with granite, doing countertops and whatever, and I had the buildings down in Wedowee that were not occupied. So, I decided to get into the granite business, which was a real fiasco.

"I had traveled to China to check out new product lines and got back two days before 9/11. It's a good thing Somebody up above was looking after me, and I didn't get hung up in China. I don't know when I would have got home.

"The granite business turned out not to be a profitable operation. The business got caught in the economic downturn of 2008-2009. It had depended on big houses being built on Lake Wedowee, but that kind of went away in the economic crisis then.

"It got to the point where they wouldn't pay any rent. The management there was not what it should have been. The biggest problem, I think, was not having the oversight there to ask questions about why this is going on. So that was a loser, and it was not a profitable business."

While the loss wasn't enough to break Floyd, he did have to close up the operation and shut the doors. In the years of economic troubles, Floyd lived by this philosophy: "I didn't borrow a lot of money. I operated on a shoestring most of the time and that was because when I first started, I didn't have any money, and I believed in hard work from day one."

Each venture he started, he started with this same frame of mind: *I don't consider myself a business guru; I just know what works.*

The businesses Floyd has opened have also provided learning grounds and employment for his family. While working with family can present its own challenges, the entire family has given Floyd a great measure of respect for his knowledge, experience, wisdom, generosity, and opportunities.

"The Wedowee Motel and Campgrounds is something I bought that I thought I could turn and make some money. So, I purchased the property and campground. It wasn't much of a campground. There were one or two little shacks on the place. I saw the potential with the growth in Wedowee around the lake. A lot of people, fishermen coming in, they needed a place to stay, and so I bought it and developed it. I built six cabins.

Floyd sporting his PF&B Developing jacket

"Then I moved little FEMA trailers in there in 2020 and made one bedroom, one bath, kitchen, and living room rental units. So, we got that monthly income coming from twenty-four rental cabins I developed on the property, plus eleven motel rooms that were already there. It provides a job for Shelly and Don Hollingsworth, my son-in-law. He manages the property for me. Cinderella Shelly, as her sisters call her because of her middle child syndrome, says my saying, 'If it's not for bedbugs, it's piss ants,' is her real-life experience running a hotel."

Floyd's satellite and side businesses also included building out townhome units in Temple, Georgia, and building a subdivision of homes in Douglasville in the decades of 2000 and 2010. He helped build houses in the Mableton area during this time as well.

"PF&B came about. It stood for Poor Floyd and Brad. Brad was a framing contractor in Temple. I got to know him, and we were talking about maybe developing some condos in Temple. So, we started a little company called PF&B and built townhouses in Temple. We probably built about thirty there. We developed a piece of property and called it Schoolhouse Trace. They were single-family condos there for the elderly folks.... They get a wheelchair through the doorways. And we went after the market of people looking for that price, it was not an expensive condo, but I think we had twenty-something units in there. When the downturn came in '97-'98, Brad filed bankruptcy, and I ended up with three or four condos to sell. It was not a money-making venture. A lot of learning; we got caught by the bad economy."

Floyd has always had respect for his humble beginnings. When asked what the PF&B stood for, he answered: "When I was on the road selling, I'd tell everybody, 'Poor old Floyd needs an order because I got a wife and four kids at home that need a meal.' It was my tagline and became my sales pitch closer. I'm not very smart, but everybody got a kick out of it. So, I used it later to keep me humble about my early hard life."

His experience in and his knowledge of millwork and the building industry, along with relationships built over the years, all worked in Floyd's favor. His ability to take a risk head-on, turn challenges into profit, and his desire to always do more are foundational pillars to every Floyd Davis venture.

CHAPTER 7

THE BIG ONE

As the storytelling sessions with Mr. Davis continued over the following weeks, I could sense a deep satisfaction in his achievements with each recollection of his past. Each story conveyed a blend of humility mixed with genuine pride in his achievements, all precisely balanced by the strength of his modest, less fortunate beginnings.

Floyd began several business ventures during his days out on the road as an independent manufacturer rep. The 127,000 miles on the road helped to build connections, relationships, partnerships, and future dreams.

It seems every life story has a big tale that almost seems too impossible to have happened. So is the case with Mr. Davis's story. Not only was Floyd busy with his travels as an independent rep for several companies, managing and running several satellite businesses of his own and now entering the manufacturing field, but he also had a huge opportunity in the Knoxville, Tennessee, area.

His growth led him to seek expansion of his operations and keep up with the demands of his growing businesses.

"In 1985, there was a company in Knoxville, Tennessee, that was a chain of about thirteen tobacco distribution plants, and in 1983, '84, and '85, there was a slowdown in the economy, and one of their facilities was up for sale.

"I got a call from Charlie Cowart. He had been working with Bass and Company, and he used to run their Knoxville branch. He said, 'There's a large facility available up here you need to come look at. If you buy it, I'll run it.' I gave it a thought, and on a Saturday, I got a couple of my friends, and we rode to Knoxville to look at this location.

"It was a 50,000-square-foot space, and Knoxville was a good location to begin expanding into production and manufacturing.

"At my first look, I wasn't too impressed. From what I've been used to at Georgia Flush Door, the machinery was outdated, there wasn't enough air going into a three-quarter-inch line to run the equipment. You could run the door machine but you couldn't run the casing cutter. It needed a lot of work to make it work for us."

Floyd purchased the Knoxville Bass and Company manufacturing space in 1985. It was a bankrupt company he bought with a 100 percent loan, which was not common in the lending industry.

"I knew the loan officer liked cowboy boots, so I bought me a pair and wore them when I went in and asked for the loan, and the loan went through! I'm not sure that this risky gesture made a difference, but it was a chance I took."

After securing the loan, Floyd began his next business step into production and manufacturing.

"So, after I bought it, I hired Charlie to run it. We got up there, and we couldn't do much production, which I'd been used to doing a lot of pre-hanging doors. And I decided that we'd go up on the weekend. I carried about three or four of my buddies with me, and we worked the whole weekend running 2-inch airlines to the machinery so we'd have enough air that we could get full production.

Floyd running 2-inch airlines to get operations up and running

"That was a long weekend and a lot of hard work, and I appreciate all them guys going with me and doing it. That's some true friends right there.

"But Knoxville at the time, the first month I bought it, we had sales of about $250,000. Of course, that's not very profitable when you do that. This was before everyone had computers. And at that time, I couldn't afford to buy the computers. They were very expensive in 1985. But what we did was put a bookkeeping system in and started up that way.

"We grew Knoxville pretty fast. The first two and a half, three years that it was operating out of the old Bass and Company warehouse, it was 50,000 square feet, and the floor was sloped toward the loading doors because it used to be a tobacco warehouse. We lost a couple of forklifts by running over the end of the 4-foot slab. But we survived.

"At the time we got the building, they didn't have a loading dock for our forklifts to load and unload. The dock was off the ground, and it was not at level with all the dock doors. So, I figured out a solution. We worked—moving, digging out of a pit—so we could back our trailers down, so it would be four feet high off the side of the building. It was big enough that I could get four loading doors in.

"We started working on that, and after I closed the building, I spent a lot of time in Knoxville running airlines, running electrical, and finishing the pit on the loading area. But just before we were getting ready to pour the slab for the 4-foot loading doors and 4-foot-high rolling doors, I got a call from Charlie on Monday asking, 'Were you supposed to pour concrete today?' He said, 'We had a heck of a rain up here over the weekend, and your block wall fell over into the pit, and you got a big mud hole out there!'

"I know what adversity is. I worked from November, December, January, and February in Knoxville. We moved into the building about March 1st."

Construction of new loading docks at old Knoxville Bass and Company warehouse

Floyd recalls a potential setback shortly after he purchased the Bass and Company space and turned it into Knoxville Door and Millwork.

"The purchase of the Knoxville Door and Millwork had a little surprise with it. After we had got opened up with the facilities retrofitted for our operations, I had a visit from the company president of Caradco Door and Windows. He flew in from their headquarters to meet with me personally to tell me they would no longer allow me to distribute their product.

"It seems that they had another company/distributor in Knoxville and did not want the competition in the area. That visit, that news made me mad and made me even more determined Knoxville would be a success.

"I told my team, 'We may not sure as hell be able to sell Caradco, but we will sure as hell show them how to sell doors!'"

Floyd faced what could have been discouraging news and a potential setback with his new Knoxville operation as a challenge, embracing it with greater confidence that this venture would succeed.

SWEDISH PLANT

Knoxville Door and Millwork opened up in the old Bass and Company space in 1985. Operations outgrew the 50,000-square-foot space quickly and left Floyd calculating his next growth move.

"I was looking for another warehouse to operate out of, and I had figured out what it would cost me to build a 160,000-square-foot building, and it was $1.8 million. I had been looking for a warehouse or a place to build one. That's when I saw this building for sale in the industrial park.

"I stopped and went in. There was a fellow there from Sweden, and it was a Swedish-owned company. He said they wanted $2.5 million for this 160,000-square-foot facility. Of course, I had already figured out what it cost me to build—1.8 million. So, I went back and talked to Charlie and made sure that we had enough money to at least put earnest money down on it. Then I called a real estate company to put in an offer, and they didn't want to write me up with a cheap-cheap offer like that—1.8 million versus 2.5 million. But I said go ahead and write the contract.

"They answered back and said, 'Well, you're gonna have to give me some earnest money.' So I called Charlie; he checked with the bank, and we had enough to give the guy the amount of earnest money he wanted.

Knoxville Door & Millwork has grown to a 165,000-square-foot warehouse and sales office.

"Well, I didn't at all think I could buy that large building that cheap, so I didn't think any more about where I was gonna get the money. But in about two weeks from the time that I made the offer, I got a call from Charlie, and he said, 'You know that building you made the offer on? You got it.' I said, 'Oh, Lord, where am I gonna get 1.8 million?'

"As it worked out, First American Bank in Knoxville made me an SBA loan. I had to put 10 percent down, and I borrowed that $180,000 from a bank in Douglasville on my signature alone, which is impossible to do this day and time!

All hands on deck helping to quickly move into a new facility

"We done the impossible in a move into that location. In one weekend, we moved all the inventory and hooked up the machinery to run to have orders ready to ship on Monday.

We shipped on that Monday $40,000 worth of doors. But we had to. I didn't have a choice. I had borrowed money based on what I sold. If I sold $100,000, I could borrow $75,000. But that was some tough times back then. I stayed up there Saturday, Sunday. I would come home about every two weeks, but that was a struggle. And then, when we moved into the building, we shut down Friday at 12:00 at the old place and started hauling inventory, all the equipment over there. And we had Jeff Smith; he was taking it off the trucks. We had already predetermined where we wanted to put the inventory.

"We done the impossible to open up on Monday morning after working Friday, Saturday, and Sunday from 10 or 11:00 at night and getting the job done. But . . . I needed the money to survive.

"It all worked out after a lot of hard work and help from my friends and everybody else I could get to work. It was a really good investment because that building was 160,000 square feet, and we got the loading docks about 80 percent finished, and we were still working on loading docks when I decided that we'd had enough that weekend. It turned out to be a very good operation. We were up there for sixteen years."

Moving inventory from the old location to the new 160,000-square-foot facility

The purchase of this massive 160,000-square-foot facility in Knoxville was a much-needed investment for Floyd. He was able to operate out of 80,000 square feet of the facility and lease the other 80,000 square feet to pay the mortgage on the entire space. This additional manufacturing space allowed him to keep up with the growth demands of the consumers and the industry trends. The door industry was shifting, and Floyd was leading the way in new trends.

Inventory relocated and ready for business

"In 1996, in the patio door business, there were a lot of 6' x 6'8" aluminum patio doors that wore out the tracks; they would wear out and the rollers wouldn't stay on the track. I had known this from working in Douglasville. So, when I was in a sales meeting on Saturday, they were talking about a retrofit patio door. Retrofit means that it was 6' x 6'8" rough opening, where a standard unit was 6'2" x 6'10".

"So, I had the idea; we started making a retrofit patio door, and the sales were great.

"I started calling on the Lowe's Company in North Wilkesboro, North Carolina, and I introduced them to a retrofit patio door. And after about six months of talking, they said 'We are gonna go with your patio door program.' That was huge.

"From that point, in 1996 and the start of '97, we developed a retrofit patio door. I had the location in Wedowee, Alabama, that we built in '93. So, we run components down in the Wedowee plant; we buy them and send them to Knoxville to build the retrofit patio door. It worked out great! We grew the business from about 1985 to the last month I operated the business; we did about $57 million in sales and was netting about 8-10 percent profit.

Door machine operation

"But that, as it turned out, was after a lot of hard work and taking all the risk. We needed to get Lowe's Company sold on the program. It helped that I had Knoxville and Wedowee working together to make it happen. Things grew so fast I then put in another plant at Muskogee, Oklahoma, and another one in Arizona just to keep up with the Lowe's sales.

"That whole time was a wild ride! Getting nationwide production and distribution for Lowe's was a major turning point. But the purchase of that 160,000-square-foot Swedish company space in Knoxville was how it all worked out. That was a big risk I took!"

Door machinery

Big risks seem to be a common thread in Floyd's stories.

"It all worked out after having realized what we had to do to keep the business but whatever it took, we did it, whether it was working on Sunday or whatever. That has always been my mindset: *Do whatever it takes.*

"I remember working out of the warehouse one day and walking into the office area looking fairly rough. I had been out helping the crews. There was this suited guy in the lobby, and I asked him 'Can I help you?' He quickly and rudely said, 'No, I'm here to meet with Floyd Davis.' I guess my appearance in work clothes was not what he expected. So, I politely said, 'You're welcome to have a seat.' Then I went through the door and out of sight. I waited a few minutes and then walked back into the lobby and introduced myself: 'Hello, I'm Floyd Davis.' That poor man backtracked every way he could, apologizing, saying he thought I was one of the warehouse workers. I can't remember, but I don't think I did business with him after realizing how little respect he showed for people of all means."

Floyd recalled a story about his encounter with his first round of workers during the time span he was building up the Knoxville manufacturing facility workforce. "When we had the Knoxville operation, I was in the back working. We were trying to build up the crew in the plant to service the global stores nationwide. We must have went through probably fifteen to twenty young men. It was hard work, tough work, and you would work up a good sweat.

"I would have these guys tell me, 'Look, I'm not gonna sweat for nobody.' So, I would tell them to 'Hit the damn road. We'll find somebody that will.' And that's what we did.

"I bought a house, the only house in this industrial park that was right across the railroad tracks from the Knoxville Door and Millwork. It was a workers' hotel, in a sense, and I would put thirty or so Mexicans in there, and we worked seven days a week with several rotating work shifts and crews. The Mexicans, they'd work six, seven days a week; it didn't matter to them. They were hard workers. If the house would have burned and killed a bunch of Mexicans, I would have been put in jail, probably still to this day! But it worked out. We did keep the Lowe's business and became Lowe's vendor of the year in 1997! I also had crews working three shifts, even overnight, seven days a week in Wedowee to keep up with the Lowe's sales demand! But it all worked out pretty good, because in 2001, I sold the business to Jeld Wen, who was a major supplier of steel doors and exterior door frames. We were contacted by Jeld Wen that they might be interested in buying us, so we decided to sell and do something else; of course, I'm sixty-seven years old at that time. I didn't get

started very early. I was close to forty when I went out on my own in 1975."

During the first years of stepping out on his own, Floyd had his hands in many business ventures. He had several small salvage door and millwork operations around the Atlanta area with BML in Douglasville as the main hub. The Cartersville, Woodstock, Norcross, and Nashville locations were established as retail stores, while Blacksburg and Knoxville were bigger operations. They were two-step operations that serviced the eastern United States. Millwork dealers would buy in bulk and sell to contractors, making for very profitable margins.

He also opened a successful sheetrock business which he sold to his partner, Bruce Armor, years later, and several other side business ventures filled Floyd's portfolio.

Floyd was also still traveling as an independent rep working with and selling products for several companies nationwide like Temple Products, JLM, and Georgia Flush Doors.

CHAPTER 8

Vendor of the Year

It wasn't long before Floyd was being noticed for his hard work and entrepreneurial gifting.

"When I quit my job at Georgia Flush Door in 1975 and went out as a manufacturer's rep, I was making some calls in Atlanta and ran across Jimmy Moore with JLM Company. They imported Honduras pine from Honduras and kiln dried and ran flat jambs out of their operation.

"Jimmy was the second company that I got to represent in the Millwork Industry. I met Jimmy Moore out making calls when I was calling Sequoia Building Supply. He came and introduced hisself, and I asked him if he needed somebody to sell his product. He said 'No. I'm going sell it myself.'

"Well, about two weeks later, he called me back up and he said, 'Hey, I think probably what I need to do is let you see if you can sell it.' So I went and visited his plant in Roanoke, Alabama.

"About the only thing he had to sell at the time was the Honduras pine flat jambs, which was not used in the area, and a lot of builders were not familiar with this pine. So, I used a little different approach to get builders that had never heard of Honduras pine. I talked to about five or six distributors in Atlanta into buying one hundred sets of them to see how it worked for them because they were about 10 percent cheaper than what their other options were. As it turned out, I increased his sales about 300 percent in the first year, but that was a lot of hard work! I had to get builders on board with the idea of using a new product, and I had done it by offering to send them a few sets of the Honduras pine doors instead of a truckload. Giving them a chance to use them before buying larger loads."

This business connection with the JLM Company began while Floyd was still traveling the roads as an independent manufacturer rep. It was early in those years on the road and one that turned out to be an open door into another great business venture; however, not without a costly twist and another opportunity for Floyd to turn a potential loss into great profits.

"After I had been repping for Jimmy Moore for about six or eight months, I visited his plant in Roanoke, Alabama, pretty often, and I noticed he had a lot of red oak around. I had an idea, and I got him in the red oak hybrid step tread business. It turned out to be a great business. We came up with a hybrid tread where the tread was red oak on about 12 inches on one side and pine on the 3-foot or 4-foot step tread other part. It made them a lot more economical to use because the end of the step that was returned where the balusters was covered up with carpet would be finished underneath with the pine that was unseen. This new design saved on the use of the expensive red oak. So, I started manufacturing what we called a hybrid step tread, which was a cross between oak and Honduras pine. It turned out to be a big market. Before I left Mr. Moore, that had developed into a great business. But in 1987, Jimmy called me up. He was having financial problems and wanted to sell me his business. So, I went to visit Jimmy and looked over his books and made a deal with him.

"He was going to take inventory, and I was gonna pay him the price of the inventory on hand, plus a salary to stay on and run the place. We had just taken an inventory, and there was a lot of oak for stair treads stacked up against the wall. Mr. Moore told me, he said, 'Those are ready to be glued up for step treads.'

"The Monday after we closed the deal, one of the sales reps called in and wanted to buy some oak step treads, and I called the shop foreman and asked, 'I've seen all that oak stacked up against the wall; can we make treads out of it?'

"This is oak that I paid about $15,000-16,000 for in the deal with Jimmy, which was supposed to be solid pieces of clear red oak, but it turned out it was only edgings! So, Mr. Moore had put one over on me on that deal! But I told him we didn't need his services no more, that we could run the place without him. So, I got him off the payroll. But that business grew into a pretty good business. In fact, we started making not only flat jambs but split jambs and casing. Anything I thought we could run in that plant to make a little money, we tried. We had a pretty good finger joint operation going where you take small blocks of wood, rip them down, and finger joint them together and run casing, jambs and whatever out of it."

Floyd had the ability to take nothing and make something of it. He turned even sawdust into dollars!

"To help with the profitability of JLM Company, we were running mouldings and split jambs and developing a large lot of shavings. We sold the shavings by truckloads to people in the chicken house business. Every time they changed out chickens, selling off the big ones, they would bring in little chicks and spread shavings in the chicken house. So, they would buy truckloads. But we weren't making much money off of it. So, I got to check into bagging shavings for the folks in Florida that had these big horse farms and horse boarding places. We started bagging shavings and we were selling them for $4 a bag instead of $30 a truckload. That was one of the little things that made JLM profitable. So, with the JLM venture, I took what looked like a huge loss and turned it into dollars.

"I did have to write the inventory down $30,000 in loss. After that big loss, I started to make split jambs to hang interior doors on. We didn't have a good source of 5/4 boards, so that's when I started buying 2 x10 short blocks from these pine sawmills. We would rip them, plane them down, and then finger joint them into a split jamb. It wasn't the best product in the world, but it worked. I called Charlie in Knoxville and told him, I said, 'Look, I don't care what they look like or what your people think, we got to use them, or we won't be in business.' So we developed that split jamb business into a pretty good business to ship into Knoxville.

"About the same time that I bought the JLM business from Jimmy, we had moved into the 160,000-square-foot building in Knoxville and had sales of $3 million a month.

"I bought the assets of JLM in 1987 and changed to DCL after I bought Jimmy Moore out. The DCL stood for Davis, Coward, and Lacey. Charlie Coward was my manager at the Knoxville branch. Brian Lacey was the manager at DCL when it was started in Roanoke, and we moved it to Wedowee in 1993. Brian Lacey was the ramrod of that business. But it turned out to be a pretty good deal for me."

Later on, when we got the business from Lowe's Company on patio doors, we brought a lot of scrap in from JLM/DCL and used it for packaging and whatever you needed to have to enhance the patio door business. That part of the business alone pulled in about 3 million each month."

Floyd helped develop new product lines with JLM while he repped for them, and in turn, he received profits twice from this business venture. First with his rep percentage of sales he made, and then the huge profits this business turned once he bought the company in 1987.

This, however, was not the only thing Floyd had his hands in at the time. In 1985, Floyd was also looking at other possibilities to expand his operations.

Floyd took JLM and established it as ProBuilt. It had its main manufacturing facility in Roanoke, Alabama, at the time. But shortly after purchasing the facility and realizing his need for expanded production space, Floyd began efforts to relocate this facility.

"While I was at JLM, I needed to learn the manufacturing end of things. The only way I knew how was to jump in. So, I ran the second shift. But we also had a first shift. So, I was in a learning curve because a lot of that manufacturing I never was exposed to. But I would go in at about 9:00 in the morning and work 'til 11:00 p.m. One night, I got a motel room right there in Roanoke. Turned out to be one that was NOT decent to stay in. Sometimes that's part of the sacrifices you have to make.

"But working those two shifts really taught me a lot about what was going on because I'd never been in the manufacturing business before. Putting my hands on it was the only way I knew I would be well-versed in it. So, the only way I knew to learn was to work both shifts and learn it all.

Governor Hunt along with state local and local officials at Wedowee facility groundbreaking

"It was kinda funny working those shifts—they, the workers—didn't realize I was the owner. They were shocked when they found out!"

As Floyd browsed through several pictures with me from over the years, he began to recall another big move.

"It turned out to be profitable to learn the entire business. After I bought the JLM Company and established ProBuilt, I moved it out of the building in Roanoke and moved it to Wedowee; that's when the city of Wedowee wanted jobs brought into the city. They donated thirty acres and the state helped me with getting a grant. The city of Wedowee put in the roads and infrastructure. We put in a 100,000-square-foot building and brought jobs to the area.

"The city of Wedowee was glad that we got a grant from the state to move our operation here. It was an ordeal to build a building. It moved from Roanoke to Wedowee in a year's time, but we accomplished that with a lot of hard work. There's a picture of the governor and everyone congratulating me for coming into Wedowee.

"We got a 30-acre piece of property from those folks and started grading on the land. I think it was in 1992, but the acreage came from the city of Wedowee. They put in the infrastructure, water lines, gas lines, all that stuff. It was on a shoestring what we were trying to accomplish. I didn't have a big crew at the time. But we all jumped in and got the job done. I had a D6 dozer down there that I put a boy to pushing dirt down there, and it was a good thing we did because about two years later, I had been working on selling to the Lowe's Company, a national program of patio doors, and that came to pass. So ProBuilt became a place to use to help in the beginning. If it hadn't been for that place in Wedowee with the patio door business as ProBuilt—that's what we call our sales group—we could not have taken on the Lowe's Companies. ProBuilt was turned into a patio door manufacturing plant.

"I had an auction and sold all the finger joint and equipment and millwork running equipment and devoted it primarily to just the patio door for Lowe's. But as it ended up, we had the plant in Knoxville making patio doors and in Wedowee. The sales were going so well, Lowe's wanted me to cover the whole US, so the next plant I opened up was in Muskogee, Oklahoma. After that, we put one in Arizona and covered the whole United States for the Lowe's Companies. We've shipped patio doors to Hawaii and Alaska. It turned out to be great! Another great business I opened and operated from 1985 to 2001. Then Jeld Wen . . . approached me about selling the company. So, we thought about it. I talked to Charlie and Mr. Beavers, our CPA, and decided we could pick up a good bit of profit on selling the business. So, I decided to sell it."

VENDOR OF THE YEAR
Floyd's can-do attitude, tenacity, and business acumen was beginning to pay off dividends.

"On that business venture ride, in 1997, we were presented the President's Vendor of the Year for the Lowe's Companies. That was a pretty big honor for me because we beat out some real big corporations, and we succeeded in getting Lowe's into the retrofit patio door business. Receiving the Lowe's President's Award for this Supplier of the Year was a pretty good accomplishment for a little ole company like ours. It all worked out. Thanks to good friends and a lot of hard work."

Floyd has had several large accomplishments and recognitions to his credit over the years. In 1997, he was nominated for Businessman of the Year for the state of Tennessee. The US Small Business Administration recognized him in 1988. Caradco recognized his contributions to the millwork industry at their annual celebration. Floyd's accomplishments throughout this time were many. But he was most proud of the move he made with his business manufacturing operations to Wedowee and the impact it made on Wedowee's economic base by providing jobs and tax base to this rural Alabama community.

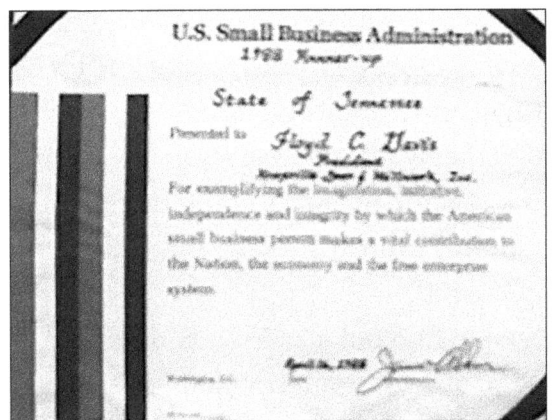

Recipient of US Small Business Award in 1988

Floyd also had the opportunity to expand the operations in Wedowee to include a sawmill and used timber from his land. He scouted out used parts to build a sawmill complete with dry kilns. This made it possible to manufacture the components for the doors and millwork for his plants.

"I found an old sawmill furnace in South Carolina. We took it down from Myrtle Beach, South Carolina, in the middle of July, me and two others. It was so hot we like to have croaked up there. But this unit was to run the boiler for the dry kiln. That was a pretty good-sized project right there. We had to unscrew all the panels off of that thing. And then build it back. I wasn't afraid to tear it down and then relocate it and rebuild it. I couldn't afford to buy a new one.

"In the warehouse, we would run sawdust through the hammer hog that would beat it up into small pieces and then run it in the boiler, the furnace. You would use your leftovers—scraps—and the hammer hog would beat up these blocks. Instead of using gas, we used scrap, so you repurposed every bit of your scrap to keep the furnace hot and boiler running. I wanted to get into the sawmill business.

"I decided that what I needed to do to get our cost down was to put a sawmill in, so we could buy red oak logs and Southern Yellow Pine and make millwork products and door components.

"As I began to find out a little bit about the sawmill business, I'd go to auctions and watch and see what they sold for. I went to an auction over in Meridian, Mississippi, and they had about the size mill that I wanted. So, I borrowed the money from the bank and bought the sawmill. That's when I built the building to operate it out of in Wedowee, and we sawed oak and Southern Yellow Pine. Then we had to kiln dry it which was fairly expensive. So, we put in dry kilns and had air drying sheds—two air drying sheds to air dry the lumber before we run it in the kilns. We had two dry kilns that would hold about 15,000 board feet of lumber each. We had to have heat out there. So, I bought a used 400-horsepower boiler from over in Mississippi and that's what we used—the saw dust to burn to make enough heat for the air drying of the kilns. We got into the sawmill business and finger joining in Wedowee—it's all still there—dry kiln sheds and drying sheds. But that was all a new venture for me. I had never been experienced in sawmills.

Vendor of the Year 107

"One thing I have always thought—that I could do whatever I wanted to. Give me a challenge and I was up for it."

The Wedowee investment turned out to be a huge operation that supported the Knoxville plant as well as the plants he had opened in Oklahoma and Arizona to meet the demands as the supplier of retrofit patio doors for Lowe's stores nationwide.

It's difficult to say which paid off, Floyd's persistence, his willingness to take risks, his drive to learn new industries, or maybe his ability to defeat challenges. Or was it possibly the teamwork of all of Floyd's qualities, knowledge, skills, and grit combined that made his success?

Floyd proved his success over and over in many business opportunities and risks he took, just like the Knoxville Bass and Company manufacturing space purchase.

Floyd had the vision for the manufacturing of both windows and doors in this space. The building needed much work for this to happen. He and several friends went up to rewire the entire plant in order to manufacture both doors and windows and, in turn, turned the old, outdated space into a profit venture.

When Floyd bought the Bass and Company business, he was determined to keep the doors open for a year; he knew it would make it if he did. This was the first of several other small manufacturing plants in Floyd's business venture portfolio.

Between the years of 1985-2000, the Knoxville Millwork business operated in 80,000 square feet of a 160,000-square-foot building in Knoxville. He leased the remaining space, bringing in more cash flow, and paid the existing mortgage on the building. The business did $65 million in sales with 10 percent profit base, and the Swedish Manufacturing Company sold for $3

Floyd's early days learning millwork in the snake pit had now earned him four manufacturing assembly plants building and shipping door and window products across the entire United States.

Jeld Wen still leases the facilities of the company Floyd sold him in 1993, and it runs over $30 million annually in production out of this little Alabama community.

CHAPTER 9

SMALL TOWN BANK AND REAL ESTATE

Since his first job in 1956, right after graduating high school, Floyd's work experience has primarily been in the millwork and construction industry. But that was all about to change when Floyd had another "idea."

SMALL TOWN BANK—1999
"Well, let's start a bank.

"Eugene Wortham had gotten fired from the Bank of Wedowee, five or six years before I really knew him. He was a neighbor. I had bought a farm that joined his, and we were baling hay one Sunday and hauling it to where I had cows over in Abernathy, Alabama. And we just got to talking about the banking business, and he's telling me he had been in it and had got fired. I said, 'Well, let's start a bank.' And he said, 'Are you crazy?'—of which I knew that I was crazy, but that's the way the idea got started.

"I told Eugene, 'Well, you find out what we got to do and how much money we need, and we'll get a bank started.'

"We had several meetings down with the Alabama Bankers in Montgomery, and they were dumbfounded as to why I wanted to take chances getting in the banking business. I straight up told them I thought we could make money in the banking business.

"So, after about six months, they gave us a charter to start the bank. We were scrambling around to sell stock, and of course, at the time, there was a lot of start-up banks going in everywhere—in Douglasville too.

"Well anyway, the Banking Commission told us that we had to have $4 million, and I was kinda confident that I wouldn't have no trouble raising that with all my buddies in Douglasville and the friends I had around that had money. I thought they'd be jumping at the chance to get into the banking business. But how wrong was I? Because what they told me, 'You don't know a damn thing about the banking business. We're gonna put our own money over here with Bill Lumpkin at First Commerce Bank and really make some money.'

"Of course, after three or four years down the road, there wasn't a bank in Douglasville that barely succeeded. But at Small Town Bank (STB), we got through that just fine. We never did have a year where we lost money except the first year that we operated. Our first six months was tight and that was not too bad a loss anyway. The second year we made profit, never did have a losing year besides the first six months of start-up.

"Back in the beginning when the regulators with the Banking Association told us you need $4 million, well, I bonused money for about everybody that worked for me to buy stock in the bank, and I sold some land to Dr. Martin—200 acres of land over there off of I-2—and I borrowed money and had Charlie buy stocks and some more people from out of town I knew, I asked to buy. They bought stocks. It was a scramble getting the entire $4 million backing investment together.

"Of course, they all praise me now because it sure turned out to be a good investment. Your stock today, of course, is taking a dive, but that's because of the California banks. If you put money in STB at the very beginning, you would have 25:1 return on the investment. For each invested dollar, you would have had twenty-five come back to you after, I believe, fifteen years or twenty years."

While Floyd may not have known much about banking, he did have years, decades now, of business experience behind him. And his shoestring budgeting, common sense business practices, and his knack to make money marched him right into another business, the world of banking.

STB branch opening in Ranburne, Alabama

"Of course, we didn't spend a lot of money on our bank buildings like a lot of people do. The old Bank of Wedowee location was started in a propane gas company building. There was a for sale sign on the building, so I called and bought the building for a bank—not a fancy building or a lot of money spent on it, but it had the safe in it. We refurbished the bank. The door was gone, but I knew where I could get one! So just rehabbed it, really. And that's how we got started in the banking business."

Floyd's STB business began in 1999 with approximately $28,000 dollars on deposit because that was the first six months operation expense you had to have on hand for start-up costs.

"We started buying branches while we were growing, because we needed deposits. And if you go back and look through the bank statements, you see we had pretty fast growth. A lot of that was due in part to the lake property here in Wedowee, up until 2008-2009. We didn't do that good those years. Most all the banks went under over in the metro areas, Carrollton, Douglasville, Paulding. But we survived over in Wedowee.

"There were a lot of sleepless nights after talking to the regulators during that '08-'09 time, and they talked to me in private and said, 'You got to get this thing straightened out, or we gonna come do what we can.' Everything I could liquidate, I did; plus I borrowed money from other assets. I had to keep the bank afloat through that time. It was some uneasy times.

"I personally bought from the bank several pieces of property that they could collect on, one of them being a local funeral home on 26 acres. The Floyd Davis Family Partnership let them buy that; it was about $500,000. But that helped the bank out too.

"The Ranburne branch, we built it. Heflin, we bought an old bank building and put our bank in it. Carrollton we bought an existing bank building, and that Carrollton branch is doing fantastic. And Paulding County we bought another existing bank, and it is exploding up there. They are making money hand over fist.

"That Paulding County Bank wasn't that old. I got it off the internet. I saw it on Sunday, because I'd been looking for a location up there, and I had seen that building was for sale. So while I was traveling with Lewis's son who was in real estate, he was gonna show me around because I didn't know my way around Paulding County. While out looking, I found the building up for sale, and it was gonna sell the next day. So, I scrambled and found out how to get on the internet. I put in a bid. We bought it for $407,000, which was a fantastic buy; it would probably cost a million to $1.5 million to build."

The STB days lasted twenty prosperous years that grew out of a local start-up bank in Wedowee, and as STB grew, it became an attractive acquisition to other larger banks.

"We were approached by Southern States Bank; actually, we were approached by several banks wanting to buy. I was thinking at my age it might be a good time to sell. So, we had several offers from different banks, but Southern States Bank kept wanting to talk to us about buying. I knew the manager who was heading up Southern States Bank had about eight or nine branches. He kept calling me early in the morning and wanting to know if I'd made up my mind because when Lewis and I went to the board meeting and met with their board about buying the bank, they had a proposal that they gave me. I acted like I wasn't interested. I said, 'That's fine.' I didn't even look at it, and I said, 'I'll get back with you.'

"After about two weeks, he started calling me in the morning at 8:00. So, I knew that he wanted to buy the bank, and he had offered, I think, $48 million for it, and so I let him stew for a day, or two or three weeks. I thought, if we could get $50 million out of it, that'd be a pretty good deal.

"The stock that I owned at STB . . . to make this deal work, it come down to I was gonna have to take more stock than I actually wanted to. But that worked out fine until the California Banks went down in 2023! But anyway, they'll be back upwards. The bank is well run. They're making a lot of money so they'll be back up.

"Now open for business" sign

"But if you went back and received all the dividends you got from STB—used to, we'd give dividends on $400-500 million each year or $1,000 each year. It was an excellent investment, made a lot of money, and is still making some money. So, if you invested $10 in a share of stock, you got back nineteen times what's reinvested, plus the dividends over the years."

As Floyd recounted these stories of his banking venture, you could sense the deep pride he felt in pursuing this "idea" he had one day out baling hay.

From July 1999-2019, STB, with its first location in Wedowee, broke even in its first year and made a profit every year thereafter. The bank went on to have six additional locations in the eastern Alabama and west Georgia area.

"Small Town Bank was an excellent risk for an old country boy who didn't know anything about banking!"

STB—1999-2019. Twenty-plus years in the making.

REAL ESTATE AND LAND INVESTMENTS

When you look at all the opportunities and investments Floyd has made over the years, one stands out as monumental—his real estate and land investments.

Over the course of decades, Floyd has purchased land and properties, and with many, he has developed commercial and residential projects. Commercial properties that have housed his business operations, residential subdivisions, retail rentals, and raw land that seemed to have no potential have all made a healthy portfolio for Mr. Davis.

"In the 1980s, my brother Mack and I bought 200 acres on Pumpkintown Road in Paulding County. We bought it for $250,000, sold it five years later for $500,000. We doubled our money and investment. Looking back, if we had held on to it for maybe another ten to fifteen years, it could have sold for millions. That's where all the commercial development in Paulding County is built up now. But it would have been worth much more if we had held on to it."

Horse Land

Floyd always kept his ear to the ground for business and investment opportunities.

"Back in the 1970s, there was talk of horse racing coming to the area. So, I got up eight investors and bought some pasture land in east Alabama. I had told some investor friends, if we buy pastureland between Birmingham and Atlanta, we could really make a mint when all these horse people come in and this horse racing takes off. So, we bought 700-plus acres and then a little recession hit, and nobody could pay their share of the payment. So, I borrowed money and started buying everybody's shares out of this setup. When we bought it, they had told me there was no timber value on it. But I would take my dog, Josie, walking on the property, and I kept seeing a lot of timber. And after getting a timber company out to take a look, they ended up harvesting more than enough to pay off the loan from this land that had no timber value! Sold enough timber off the track to pay for the whole dang thing!"

Subdivisions and Condos

"I built Willow Bend Sub in Douglasville. That was a risky project. It was 'on the other side of the tracks' as they used to say, up on the north side of Douglasville in a lower income range of homes. It proved to be a good project and helped the community out on that end of town.

"That's when I bought some condos in Panama City.... I had POFA and POFF—Poor Old Floyd Florida and Alabama—and that's when the condos down there ended up with, I think it was four or five. Emerald Isle was the first one I bought. I had a great duplex down there I bought in 1988. I still own that one. The rest of them have been sold. I had them for probably ten years. Today I've got the brick duplex still under a rental contract for $1,700 a month. I have income coming in off that brick duplex. Before I decided to start renting it, I would let anybody go down there that wanted to. I think Shelly would go down for weeks at a time. Jacob, her third oldest, he would complain about his mama making him pull their cooler or whatever they took through the sand. He said, 'That's tough work!' She stayed on him all the time, but he had to tote everything to the beach, and he still comments to me to this day about how 'Mom made me do this and that.' She helped him learn tough love, just like my mama taught me.

"I remember when me, Angela, three or four kids, and our friend John Crawford let me go down to his little house. It was a blessing. Otherwise, we wouldn't have got to go to Florida, and I felt the same way about letting folks go down anytime. I never did charge anybody until I put it up for rent through a leasing agency back three years ago."

As we discussed his real estate endeavors, Floyd seemed to light up and get excited about all he had invested in over the years and what it meant for his future and his family's inheritance.

"I have property in Douglas and Heard Counties that both have big potential, all because I bought some dirt, held on to it, and it has turned out to be in some good locations. In Douglas County, there is a guy from Saudi Arabia looking to purchase a large tract I own off of Highway 5 past the roundabout and bring in tech and manufacturing. In Heard County, I have another commercial tract with several potential offers in the market."

Reflecting on his real estate ventures, Floyd emphasized there have been too many transactions from buying and selling, rental income, and development to recall them all. In 2001, he sold ProBuilt Knoxville and Wedowee businesses. However, he retains the property ownership and income generation from those properties.

Floyd's latest real estate venture is his local investment in his own home community of Heflin, Alabama.

"The beginnings of infrastructure are going on now. Over 4,000 acres I have purchased in the last several years by buying up adjoining tracts of land. I now own an entire mountain and surrounding land. The property is beautiful with both mountain views in every direction and riverfront property in the valley area. It's a gorgeous piece of property, that when the market turns again, will be marketed nationally, and maybe globally as a premiere development to the right investor. It will bring in big dollars and will put Heflin, Alabama, on the map!"

CHAPTER 10

A Chat With Lewis Beavers

Some friendships and relationships formed over a lifetime stay with you for life. They accompany you on your journey—sometimes guiding, sometimes simply offering companionship, and at other times, standing by your side as you weather life's storms. Lewis Beavers is one such friend for Floyd.

While Floyd and Lewis's friendship began as a business-client relationship in 1975, their almost fifty-year journey together expands beyond the account books and business record keeping. Lewis has offered Floyd more than financial services; he has helped Floyd to maneuver through his business ventures with the sole purpose of protecting Floyd's assets as his own. Lewis is not only Floyd's CPA but a close, personal friend.

In the early years as Floyd's businesses began to expand in multiple locations and grow beyond just retail sales into the production and manufacturing fields, Floyd recognized the need for someone to help manage and keep track of his expanding business ventures.

Floyd and Lewis sat down to share their story for "the official record." Floyd recalls:

"I met Mr. Beavers when I was looking for a CPA in Douglasville. I didn't meet him when I first went in; I think I met Ollie Robbins, and then after he retired, of course, me and Mr. Beavers have been working together coming up on fifty years."

Lewis added, "The office there in Douglasville, when we purchased it, the gentleman there before had been ill for a couple of years. The practice dwindled down. So, either myself or Ollie would meet clients in the Douglasville office one or two days a week as the business grew there in Douglasville.

"Since I live close to that office, I started spending more and more time there rather than our Atlanta office. And that's really when I guess I got involved with Francis from your office. I didn't see much of Floyd. He was out and about, but Angela would come in and bring the bookkeeping in or have one of the girls run it in and drop it off.

"I guess we really got involved, at the beginning of Knoxville because it required more involvement in the accounting and auditing part of the business. We started spending more time together as he expanded in the various locations, and also in different projects, whether it be construction or home building. I was involved in that as far as helping get those up and going."

Floyd interjected, "It just sort of evolved from that to a whole bunch of new adventures. The first venture would have been the little building we leased across the street from the Wickes

A Chat With Lewis Beavers

Lumber Company on Highway 78. They were a big chain of retail lumber dealers, and I thought that people going in their building would see my little place and then check us out. So that worked out good, being across the street from the Wickes.

"Now Darcy was the first to work there. She was probably fifteen or sixteen. She cried, of course, having to be there, but I was just down the street about two blocks. So, if she had a problem, she could call me. Shelly worked there too. They did stay by themselves, and they learned the business at a very young age. Darcy left to go to college, and then Shelly ran the place. They both learned by the same process, learning while trying to. That place across from Wickes was one of my first salvage locations in what I called the junk business."

Lewis recalled other details. "Well, what I remember when Floyd came in the first time, he actually met with a partner of mine as a new client. He told me who he was; of course, I didn't know Floyd at the time, and he said he was in the junk business. The way Floyd described the junk business, he would buy these seconds, doors and stuff, fix them up, and sell them. So that's the first of those Douglasville operations that I remember—we call it the junk business."

"My first buy on inventory was a couple hundred wood fir exterior doors for sale that were damaged," said Floyd. " I had been working millwork up in Myrtle Beach, South Carolina, and ran across this man selling seconds. He called me up because he had heard I had gotten into the junk business, and he said he had some doors but wanted to know if I could pay in cash. I said, 'What do you want for them?' He wanted $978, which was a heck of a buy. So that was my first purchase of inventory; it was from Charlie Yett, and he is still alive. I talk to Charlie probably three or four times a year.

"But that's the way we got started with the first inventory, and then I traveled as a manufacturer's rep, and I was always running across deals where somebody was changing window brands and they had excess windows or doors or whatever that I could buy at about 20 percent of the original cost, so you can make real good profit on that junk."

"That junk business, however, we laugh about it now, but it jump-started you into several different things," Lewis noted. "Knoxville would be, I guess, the next big move? Although you did get into the sheetrock business before Knoxville over in Woodstock. Then from the sheetrock you met Charlie through your manufacturer rep travels ... Charlie Cowart.

"The Knoxville location, it was owned by Bass and Company, and they had filed bankruptcy. And Charlie called Floyd and says, 'You know, you need to come up here and look at this place,' and Floyd thought it was a good opportunity. That would have been in early '85. They opened—I remember this date—because they opened it, or purchased it April 15, 1985. Of course, that is tax day!

"It was an old tobacco warehouse. The floors were sloped to drain out as the tobacco dried. It needed some work."

Floyd added, "We lost a few forklifts off the dock; it slanted but it was on two different levels, and it really wasn't conducive to doing the millwork business or manufacturing or assembly."

Lewis then recalled, "He was moving materials. Handling inventory two or three times when it should only be handled once. Just because of how the building was laid out."

"Right after I first bought it," said Floyd, "I got up there, and I was trying to figure out how we could increase production because they were a Caradco distributor, who is a major window distributor, and when I bought the Bass and Company, I thought that I would get the Caradco line. But to my surprise, I did not. There was some pressure put on Caradco by the new owner of Georgia Flush Door. They had a Caradco distributor in Nashville and didn't want the competition. He was not in Knoxville, but I got shot out of the saddle on that one. For sure."

Knoxville facility loading dock construction

Lewis added, "And that was an important play, because that was a big percentage of the sales in this operation. It looked like it could potentially be a huge financial setback."

Floyd agreed. "Yes, 30-something percent of the sales at the time. So, after I found that out, I thought and told my team there, 'Well, we can't sell Caradco windows; I'm gonna show them how to sell doors!'

"So that was the time we went up there, ran new air lines, and got this huge plant outfitted with lines that was big enough to run the exterior door machine and the casing cutter. I gathered up a crew on the weekend, went up there, and run 2-inch airlines all over the warehouse so we could get some production. That was, I think, six or eight friends that went with me to help do that. But we started to really push in the exterior door units and interior door units. I told my sales team, 'Don't miss any orders on doors.' So, we got the sales force back that we had lost when the business sold. We had a really good sales representative over the road. And if I remember right, we didn't lose much money in the first year."

"If so, it wouldn't be much, if any, the first year, and then after that, it showed a profit every year thereafter," said Lewis. "That is typically unheard of for a startup. It takes a three-to-five-year window to get to where you're actually making money. That was in '85 and the end of '86 when you bought the Knoxville building in that industrial park."

Knoxville facility overhaul work

"And that was a big gamble for me because when we bought the building, I didn't have one red cent invested in it," said Floyd. It was borrowed money from an SBA loan, and then Bob Stewart from the bank in Douglasville, he loaned me $180,000 on my signature, and that's unheard of these days! And then that next month, I sold a piece of property I had in order to pay Bob back. Tough times back then."

Lewis remarked, "That operation moved right at the end of '86 to the new location, and you moved in that business in one weekend, which was quite an accomplishment. You knocked it out because you had to ship it and sell it on Monday."

"Yeah," replied Floyd, "we shipped 40,000 that Monday, but we didn't have a choice. We needed the money, and I had borrowed money based on 75 or 80 percent of sales. So, I had to have the sales; it was a struggle up there for six or eight months, but I think we made money the year we moved. In fact, I don't know if we ever lost money in the year up there. Don't think we ever lost money."

Lewis confirmed what Floyd remembered.

As the conversation with Floyd and Lewis continued, they began to tell of the days when Floyd experienced high interest rates in some hard economic times.

Floyd said, "I really never was afraid of not succeeding. I don't remember being afraid of interest rates. I know when we bought the Knoxville operation, if I remember right, the interest rate was around 10 percent."

Lewis thought about that. "Let's see, in that same timeframe construction loans were at one time with inflation really high. There in Jimmy Carter's days."

"Yeah, well, I had some houses with construction loans as high as, you know, 21 percent," Floyd replied.

Lewis recalled, "You had some houses with owner finance mortgages of 12-14 percent and some 16 percent."

Floyd reminisced and enthusiastically proclaimed the miracle of it all. "We look back now, and ask, how did that happen? How do you make money in those terms, given what we know today as far as interest rates and home mortgage rates, but the difference was people bought the houses and they could afford them, right? Even with those high rates."

Lewis mused, "Not so much government involvement."

Floyd said, "I know some months in Knoxville, we had a customer who'd buy our damaged and salvaged doors, and he'd pay cash. We got a junk safe to keep the cash in, and I would take some cash from Knoxville and pay some of the notes. I also owner-financed several 30-year mortgages. I had spent $800,000 that I had to make to get out of a trap."

"When it got tight, though, the way to sell the houses was the owner financing," added Lewis. "But I don't recall you having to repo any of it."

Floyd clarified, "Most of them paid out. When interest rates now got better, they went out to refinance. Yes, they got paid off, some with a handshake."

This time of reflection, as Floyd and Lewis recalled past experiences, offered deeper insight into the magnitude of obstacles Floyd faced in his business ventures over the years.

Floyd continued, "I can't remember how many, but I bought a subdivision that was put in in the early '70s that just sat there. It had sewage run, along with all the infrastructure. But when the economy just stopped, the contractor lost it to their bank. I bought it from a bank. It was a 100-lot subdivision development that I bought for about $1,000 a lot. I had to spend some money, though, because people went in there and stole the covers off the sewer system, and I probably spent about that much more money getting it straightened out. That was in Douglasville, Willow Bend subdivision. It was amazing. I didn't really have the money; it just all worked together and worked out."

This story again revealed a business opportunity that Floyd took a risk on and turned into dollars. The fact that he paid $1,000 per lot, recouped somebody else's misfortune, and was able to turn the losing situation around captures the ongoing fortune Floyd accrued in his lifetime.

Lewis commented, "With all that success, there have been failures along the way too. The sawmill in Honduras is one that didn't pan out, and there's been other different things along the way that he's never been afraid of trying something and then soon get into it and realize that this may not work."

"I can think of a few specifics, but for the most part things always seemed to work," said Floyd.

Lewis said, "He was gonna get into the bonding business at one point. I initiated that. I think it was politics with the sheriffs at the time; that didn't pan out."

"So there's been several messed-up things that I've tried that didn't work," Floyd confirmed. "What I can say—it seemed to be the ones where I didn't run it myself. The ones I invested money in and let someone else run it is where I lost any money, but any business that I bought and personally ran myself never lost any money."

Lewis observed the qualities in Floyd that contributed to his success: "Floyd's always been, I guess, a risk taker, a gambler. The way I looked at it, he sees the big picture and says, 'Yeah, this could be something.' Whereas I look for the details of how you're gonna do it! So, over the years, that helped, to bat it back and forth between us. Once he shows me the big picture . . . yeah, that makes sense. Floyd's not afraid of taking a risk!"

"Not when you start from where I did, Lewis. There ain't no risk; there's nothing to lose! I can't go back to eatin' beans and cornbread."

Your Earnings Record at a Glance

Years You Worked	Your Taxed Social Security Earnings	Your Taxed Medicare Earnings	Years You Worked	Your Taxed Social Security Earnings	Your Taxed Medicare Earnings
1953	$ 445		1978	$ 17,700	$ 17,700
1954	957		1979	22,900	22,900
1955	1,384				
1956	2,668		1980	25,900	25,900
1957	3,350		1981	29,700	29,700
1958	4,095		1982	27,851	27,851
1959	4,711		1983	35,700	35,700
			1984	37,800	37,800
1960	4,800		1985	39,600	39,600
1961	4,800		1986	42,000	42,000
1962	4,800		1987	43,800	43,800
1963	4,800		1988	45,000	45,000
1964	4,800	Medicare began	1989	48,000	48,000
1965	4,800	in 1966			
1966	6,600	$ 6,600	1990	51,300	51,300
1967	6,600	6,600	1991	53,400	99,055
1968	7,800	7,800	1992	55,500	130,200
1969	7,800	7,800	1993	57,600	135,000
			1994	60,600	761,923
1970	7,800	7,800	1995	61,200	393,438
1971	7,800	7,800	1996	62,700	483,227
1972	9,000	9,000	1997	65,400	692,165
1973	10,800	10,800	1998	68,400	512,576
1974	13,200	13,200	1999	72,600	381,424
1975	14,100	14,100	2000	76,200	381,654
1976	3,060	3,060	2001	80,400	161,979
1977	16,500	16,500			

Floyd's earnings statement

CHAPTER 11

HEART OF GOLD

Floyd has a side that many don't know about, and that is his heart of gold. Both he and Angela have opened their hearts and their home to many people over the years. Floyd has always deemed it important to help those less fortunate and in great need.

Such was the case with a nearby neighbor of his, JC.

"JC Gary, he lived about a half a mile from us on a dirt road going out to Campbellton Road. JC was blind, his dad was blind.... and he worked at a broom factory over in Atlanta. It was right around the corner from where I worked. So, I started taking JC back and forth to work. We worked about the same hours, eight to five.

"JC worked in that broom factory in Atlanta for years for a meager hourly rate. This was his only means to provide for his family. He was an amazing man. I didn't know any blind folks; blind people could do as much as we could do. You'd walk in the house, it would be pitch dark, and they wouldn't have any lights on, and you'd wonder how they would eat or cook or whatever. JC had an old car out there they worked on, changed the brakes on it by feel. It just amazed me what he could do.

"Over the years I carried him to work. I worked off Moreland Avenue, and the broom factory he worked at was close by, so I would give him a ride to work every day and then pick him up on my way home."

For years, Floyd would carry JC to and from work expecting nothing in return. Angela, Floyd's wife, had learned one year that the power had been cut off for lack of payment and Floyd, while struggling to make his own family bills, paid JC's electric bill so they would have power and a warm house.

"Angela told me one day—it was sometime in the winter because I remember it was cold out. She said JC's power had been cut off because he couldn't pay the bill. So, Angela and I decided we would pay it to help him out. Now, paying our own bills was tough at the time, but somehow, we managed to pull together enough to pay for his power along with all of our own bills."

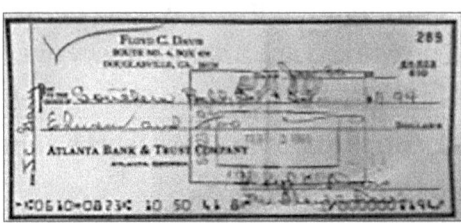

1969 check issued to pay JC's bill

Floyd recalls an event on a ride home in a colored section of town that shook both him and JC up and left them both rattled.

"I had picked him up one afternoon; it was in the summertime. We were on Capitol Avenue, it was the colored section of town, that's about all that lived there. I left Georgia Flush and picked up JC. We were stopped at a red light, and it changed to green, and as I started off, a little black child, probably seven or eight, runs out in front of me and the car bumped her and that scared JC and me both to death because there was probably fifty or sixty Blacks that came up and was hollering and carrying on. The police came and everything settled out. The little girl wasn't hurt. I never will forget that ordeal."

At this point, Angela chimed in as she recalled the poignant memory of caring for JC. "Remember the time I took him down to interview for that job?" she asked Floyd. "When you walked with him, you had to tell him when you went down the steps. We had to come up these big old steps like the Capitol, in Atlanta. When we came out of the building, we were so excited that he got the job that I forgot to say 'steps!' And just as he started to step down, I screamed, 'Steps!' but it was too late, and we rolled down them steps on top of each other, with people screaming and hollering all around us. But neither one of us got hurt."

Floyd replied, "The good Lord was looking after you both."

Floyd's generous heart was always to serve someone in need. Angela recalled, "We had a boy live with us, Jimmy Cash, who stayed with us and went back to school. We had a lot of people stay with us, and we helped along the way." While he is quite subtle about his generosity, those who have been touched by his giving hand and heart have reaped a harvest they did not labor for.

Heritage

During our conversation, one particular memory stood out to Floyd.

"When I made the trip with my grands to show them Hanging Dog and my place of heritage, I was able to make a sizable donation to the Hanging Dog cemetery for perpetual care. I have a lot of ancestry there and felt it important to help out that little community.

"As I look back over my life, I know I have been blessed, and I feel it's important to remember where you have come from and help those less fortunate. Hanging Dog is still just a small, simple community."

Hitchhikers

Trip to Hanging Dog to present funds for perpetual care

As Floyd and Angela shared these stories, you could sense a deep humility about him. His modest words were filled with much honor. He believes he has been gifted with a unique ability to face a challenge and succeed. He also believes life is better shared helping those in need.

"At the time we lived in the apartment that we rented, and I wasn't making much money at all, I had quit my job and went to TP Lumber Company where a bunch of BS was shot at me about how great this job would be. Anyway, they had a line of plywood and particleboard plaques or something that I was trying to sell, and I didn't have any money to take with me to Chattanooga. The first... client wanted to stop for a cup of coffee. Of course, I didn't have one red cent to buy him a cup of coffee."

"I did get an order from him though for half a carload of junk that was really no good, but on the way home coming down I-75 right out of Chattanooga, it was about getting dusk, and there's two kids hitchhiking. They look to be sixteen or seventeen. I stopped and picked them up and started talking to them. They had run away from home. So, I carried them to our little apartment. Angela fed them some pinto beans and cornbread.

"That's about all the staples we had. But I didn't have the money to send them back. I did take them and found them a job at the carwash, and they worked for a week or two, and got up enough money to put them on the bus and send them back home to their mom.

"I had sent a letter to their mama and told her they were okay and working to get enough money to come home. They did, and I remember their mama being so relieved we had taken them in and helped them out. I just thought, *What if that had been one of my kids? What would I want for them?* It's really just that simple with life. Be kind."

Dalton Martens

Angela shared a fond memory of a young man whom she and Floyd had the privilege to know.

"We have been knowing him [Dalton Martens] and his family since he was just five or six. I was close to his mother, and he came and lived with us for a long time. His mom and daddy were getting very old. He was their youngest son, and he worked for Floyd. So we've had a lot of people over the years that we've got really close to. Floyd is humble enough that he didn't want to toot his own horn, but he's helped a lot of people out in a lot of situations over the years.

"Floyd, he worked his whole life trying to take care of me and the kids and everybody else that needed it. And he never got to enjoy hunting or fishing like other men would. He always made sure me and his family were taken care of. He would have made sure the kids and grandkids had what they needed. He always looked for someone in need and helped. And he doesn't brag on himself."

Floyd teased, "I'm a silly old man."

Angela lovingly retorted, "He tells me all the time he's a silly old man, and I tell him, I'd much rather have a silly old man than a grumpy old one!"

Jeff Smith

Another memorable relationship Floyd had was with Jeff Smith.

Floyd shared, "Jeff Smith was a young man that I first met when he was working at Georgia Flush Door after I left there. They hired him to work in the shop. That was in probably 1977 that he went to work at Georgia Flush Door. I needed to take Douglasville and make it more high production millwork because we were chasing apartment jobs in Atlanta. He had been working for someone like Georgia Flush Door for a long time and had experience in the door business. So he came to work for me in 1984. Then when I bought Knoxville Millwork, I needed him in Knoxville because he was experienced in high-production door and door machinery, and he worked with me up there until I sold the business, and then he moved back to Alabama and he still works for me now helping to run the Millwork place here in Heflin. That's almost a forty-year working relationship."

Mr. Blythe

Though there are countless relationships that marked Floyd throughout his journey, he couldn't help but end with Mr. Blythe.

"In our early days together, if it hadn't been for him, don't know how we would have made it. He let us have milk on credit or our kids would have went hungry a bunch of times. I had $300 credit with Mr. Blythe at the store and no money to pay him, and it was a year and a half or two before I got the money to take back to him. If it hadn't been for him and him giving us that credit, our kids would have been without milk and went hungry a lot of times.

"The next time I went to the store, he called me and took me to the very back of the store and said, 'You see these little bitty shoulders?' I just nodded my head. He said, 'They can't carry the weight of the world, and you remember that the rest of your life.'

"We did pay back the $300, we sure did," Floyd said. "I wish we had remained close friends. He got killed when he was opening up the store and tripped holding the cash drawer. Fell and broke his neck, and he never got over it. I went to Crawford Long Hospital the day before he died. He was in a lot of pain.

"He was good to us. He would come by Georgia Flush Doors, and I would sell him those damaged doors, and he would take them to Douglasville and put them in the little general store out there."

Angela reflected, "We've met some wonderful people over the years and have some close friends."

"We sure have," Floyd joyfully agreed.

These are only a handful of people that Floyd's heart and hands have helped over the years. There are countless others. His humble beginnings have always fueled his desire to be there for others in time of need. Such was the case with his birth dad, Joe.

"When Joe, Floyd's real dad, was up in years and his health failing him, Floyd took care of him financially," Angela recalled. "He paid his hospital bills. He visited Joe in the hospital and paid for his burial. That says a lot about the kind of man Floyd is. He never really had his dad in his life, but he still honored him to the end in his last days. How many men would do that? My Floyd did!"

CHAPTER 12

The Love Story

They say behind every good man is a good woman. I believe Floyd would agree this holds true in his case. Floyd was quite smitten with Angela ever since the first day he met her.

Floyd and Angela's 60th anniversary celebration

On September 18, 1959, Floyd and Angela Sewell exchanged wedding vows at the young, tender ages of twenty-two and seventeen. He was with one of his friends who had his eye on Angela when they stopped by her house one afternoon.

Floyd's friend wanted to ask Angela out, but she had no interest in him. Floyd remembers the long plaid skirt and dark sweater she had on the day they met. He felt confident Angela would agree to a date, so he asked her out and, as they say, the rest is history. Floyd and Angela would have celebrated sixty-four years of marriage September 18, 2023.

I had the pleasure of sitting down with both Floyd and Angela as they reminisced over their early courtship days and their many memories of the last several decades.

Floyd started, "So, my friend Alan and me were on our way to Douglasville; he had told me he wanted me to meet his new girlfriend."

Angela chimed in, "He hadn't even asked me for a date."

"No, but he was thinking you was gonna be his girlfriend," Floyd corrected. "When I met her, I remember to this day what she had on. She had a black sweater with a pleated skirt down to her ankles with saddle oxfords and bobby socks rolled up."

"I thought, *That's the prettiest little thing I've ever seen.* I shot my friend out of the saddle on that one."

"I found out about that was on my seventy-fifth birthday," Angela said. "He told me in front of everybody. I didn't know that Alan even liked me; I thought he was just a friend."

"I've known Bonnie, my best friend, since we were born, nearly. Her daddy and my granddaddy were best friends. She always said she didn't know what Floyd had that no other guy had that ever tried to date me. But he had it!"

Amused, Floyd exclaimed, "Whatever I had, I don't know!"

"It was his kindness, and he was sweet and handsome," Angela answered.

That first encounter was in 1958. Floyd and Angela dated about a year before he asked for her hand in marriage.

"On the honeymoon, on the way home the next day, we had about $20 to $25 left," Floyd recalls. "That was the one reason we didn't go on to the mountains; we didn't have the money, but we stopped in Mableton by Leland Heights grocery store and got about $20 worth of groceries, which was five bags full at that time. We even bought a bread bin that we still got, still use. That was quite an experience for me. Then we moved into our little house with no water, no doors or well. That was some good memories."

Early dating years

Angela recalls the innocence of their honeymoon night, as they both grinned and laughed about their early days. "He was like, 'Do you want me to put these on?' He had never slept in pajamas, but we were both just young and dumb, like I said, about everything. I said, 'Yes, I'm going to put my trousseau nightgown on,' so I put on this long gown down to my ankles. It had a big ole sash, and I tied it. We got in the bed like we knew what we were doing, and we didn't know nothing! But that was always funny to me—to us. And like I said, he was always kind and gentle and sweet, so he didn't scare me at all."

Angela does recall one story from their dating days: "My mom was afraid he was a wild boy because he had been over at the house one night and when he left the house, he had to come back to borrow money from Mama to pay a fine to keep from going to jail."

The two of them both looked at each other, grinned, and laughed as they shared this memory.

"I had left her house and was going down by what they call the black cabins—it's a little eating place and I had a '55 Chevrolet, and I thought I was a badass. So going by the little joint there, I threw it up in second, and *vroom, vroom,* I had glass packs on the car, so it was loud.

"What I didn't know was that the state patrol was sitting there. So, they gave me a ticket. Blue lights in my rearview and all! We didn't have cell phones back then, so I drove back to her house to borrow the money from her mother to pay the fine. I think it was about $20. It wasn't that much, but $20 was a lot of money back then."

"Mother let him borrow the money to keep from going to jail. And, she let me keep dating him," Angela added, delighted.

ANGELA'S FAMILY

Angela's family had given Floyd their stamp of approval, treating him like their own. Floyd began the story.

"Angela's granddad shoed horses and mules. He had a little blacksmith shop out beside the house, and he shoed horses for Mac Abercrombie who had a horse barn in downtown Douglasville years ago. Abercrombie was the sheriff at the time. I would go up to his horse barn and help her granddad shoe horses, and he would bring these little wild horses in from Louisiana and put a nose twist on 'em, and I would hold the horse's head while he tried to shoe them. But that was my first experience with horses."

Angela described her mother as a "sweet woman," and Floyd agreed.

"I spent the night with them before we got married . . . and they had a bedroom with an old feather bed in it," Floyd recalled. "And her grandmother came in there—they had heat stones in front of the fireplace—and they would keep your feet warm. But she had me covered up so tight I couldn't even wiggle."

"They liked Floyd a lot," Angela said.

"I would split wood for them. I was used to working and so every time I would go out there, I would make sure they had enough firewood."

Floyd and Angela in front of her grandparents' house

A few tragedies struck Angela's home and family when she was very young. Her dad died suddenly when she was only seven months old, leaving her mama alone.

Angela recalled the details. "Mother, she was left with two little girls. My sister's daddy died with a heart attack before she was born. He had went to Covington to get a tractor or something—he had a farm, too—and he had a heart attack, and I remember that clear."

"But your dad died when you were seven months old," Floyd stated.

"I was about four and a half, I think, when Daddy Putman died," Angela added. He was my stepdad my mama married. Well, he was very good to me. My grandparents were Emerson Cook and Mayme Sailors Cook. Floyd and I spent a lot of time with them. They were very good to us, and Floyd was always kind and helped them too."

STARTER HOME

In 1958, just before meeting Angela, Floyd bought his first house. Sitting on the corner of Pope Road and Lake Monroe Road in Douglasville was a 20 x 24 house that had been abandoned. It needed much work, but for the asking price of $2,400, Floyd believed it to be a good deal. He had the down payment of $500 and secured a loan for the remaining balance with a promise to repay within five years. Despite a modest income of just $240 a month at Harbor Plywood, Floyd set out to make home improvements and remained committed to repaying the loan.

Starter home on Lake Monroe Drive in Douglasville, Georgia

"I paid everyone I owed. There might be times the payment was late, but I paid. It was important to me that you could count on me to pay off my debt."

"Now the first house I bought was in Douglasville, Georgia. I was dating Angela and bought a little Jim Walter house for $2,400. It had no bathroom, no doors, no water. It was sitting on block with very little insulation, and it was very cold. That's when Angela and I got married about six months later. That was our starter home.

"When we moved in, we had no running water. So, I went to digging a well. I was trying to dig a well to get us running water . . . and put a pump in it. While I was digging out the mud, the way those open buckets made the mud come up, it hit the side of it, and it would sling over and covered me up with mud, like a mud turtle. My mama came out, and I was working on that well. I made me a winch out of a piece of pine log and rope to let the bucket down. I would get somebody to let the bucket down, I would fill it up, and then they pulled the bucket back up. With me being at the bottom of the well, that bucket would hit the sides, and I would have mud splash all over me.

"Mama came out that day. It was on Sunday. I was working on the well and she started boo-hooing when she saw what I was doing.

"When I finally got the well done, the sides started caving in on it. So, I rounded me up some concrete pipe and let it down into the well. It wasn't too good of a well. After all that work, we realized we didn't have enough water for it to really work right. So, I got up enough money to get a well drilled.

"Off down in the back next to the trash pile, the kids liked to see me burn the trash because there were aerosol cans that would blow up, and they thought that was great. I'm sure Darcy remembers some of that.

"To get a bathroom in the house, of course, I didn't have the money to call a plumber; I just knew we needed a bathroom. I'd go around to the houses being built and look at how the plumbing went. 'Course, in those days, it wasn't PVC plastic. It would have made it a lot easier if it was, but it was cast-iron pipe, and you packed compound around the joints and then poured heated lead on it. Angela would help me. We'd both be under the house with a blowtorch on an iron cup. We didn't have a lead pot, but we heated up a cup at a time. It's a wonder we ain't dead from inhaling all those lead fumes, but we survived.

"I needed to add on to the house, so I took two weeks of vacation and ordered $1,300 worth of lumber, brick, plywood, and sheetrock all at one time. I didn't know you're supposed to do that in stages. I bought me a $65 skill saw and dug the footings for the block, poured them, got my lumber started, got the two-by-eight band around it. And in two weeks' time, I had that house dried in. I worked about twenty hours a day doing that. I had one gentleman down the street—he was probably in his seventies—he was the only help I had on building that thing.

"But I know what got me was when I was gonna build a little gable porch over the front. Me trying to figure out how to cut on that gable to get it to go from a 3/12 to a 4/12 pitch was a sight. Anyway, I finally figured out that roof pitch. It wasn't the prettiest job that anybody ever done, but it worked. And that's when we closed off the front of the house, and we had to hand the kids through the 28 x 46 bottom sash of the window. We had to do that because the door wasn't framed just yet. But thank goodness that didn't last too long. I remember the kids pretending to be asleep, so we would have to carry them and hand them through the window. They thought that was a thing."

Starter home addition work

The Lake Monroe house in Douglasville was Floyd and Angela's starter home. They began their life together in that place, creating many memories as they started their marriage and family there. Floyd recounted a few of them.

"We had two or three experiences out there, young folks just getting married. The front door had a glass door on the front of it, and she went outside; I locked her out. I wouldn't let her in, so she picked up a rock and threw it through the door glass. That was some of that early marriage stuff.

"I also remember there in this house that I was going to work on one morning, and we got in an argument. I threw my cup down in the hall and broke it. Well, she proceeded to get everything out of the cabinet and threw it down to the floor and broke it. We didn't have too much to start with. But that's just some of the things I remember about our first days in the little house and young married days.

"One Sunday, she went to visit her mother or something, and I had the windows to put in, so I had to take the door out and when she came back, I had the whole front of the house gone. I got it put back that day, but that shocked her; she still reminds me of that. But after I closed that front door in, we had to run the kids in and out of a window because I didn't have time to fix the door where it was supposed to go. Darcy still remembers that. I think they probably pretended like they were asleep so I would carry them in. But that's the way kids are."

Not having one tool to his name, Floyd set out and bought a skill saw, went to the local hardware store, and placed the building material order he would need to complete a 720-square-foot addition. The $1,300 needed for this space he paid for in cash. Taking vacation time off work, he spent every waking minute building on that addition and had it dried and ready for the roof within two weeks.

"I didn't know the first thing about construction work. I didn't own a single tool, but I didn't let that stop me. I took that saw and made it work, and in two weeks, I had that place dried in."

Spoken with confidence and a lingering hint of amazement at this accomplishment, Floyd shared these stories of preparing this little house to be his family's first home.

A GROWING FAMILY

Before long, the Davis family experienced the challenges of balancing a thriving business with parenting when their oldest daughter, Darcy, was born.

"Darcy, our first child, was born one year to the day after we got married. She was born on our anniversary.

"I worked at Zuber Lumber Company at that time and also worked at Wilson Freight Line on Friday nights. So, I'd get off at 5:00 on Friday and go home, see Angela, and eat supper and had to be at Wilson Freight Line at 12:00. My job was as the freight buggies came around on a track with the freight in them, whatever that buggy door number had marked on it, that was the door number it was supposed to go to. I'd pull it off by myself and roll it in the trailer and stack it up, if I could pick it up. They shipped a lot of clothes, so they were big boxes of clothes, and they were very heavy. That's where I learned hard work, well before that, too, but that was really hard work working by yourself.

"The weekend that Darcy was born, I had worked on Friday at Zuber Lumber Company. I worked Friday night over at the Freight Line, and then Mac, my half-brother, was doing a little remodeling out in Adamsville, and I went up there and worked all day to help him out and then headed home. I got home about 5 or 6:00 in Douglasville and sat down on the couch and dozed off. About five minutes later, Angela shook me and said she is having some labor pains, that we better go to the hospital in Atlanta. So, we got in the car and headed toward Atlanta. It was after 7:00 when we got there. I got her checked in. We got there between 7 or 8:00 at night, but she didn't have Darcy until the next day around 12:00.

"I'm sure I looked pretty rough after being up for three days straight and not shaved. I was asleep out in the chair in the hospital waiting room and when my mama, Roxie, came in, she told Angela I was asleep out there, and Angela said, 'Don't wake him up. He has not had any sleep tonight.'"

Darcy, oldest of Floyd and Angela's four children, was born in 1960—one year to the day after they were married. And while Darcy was fourteen months old, still in diapers, along came child number two, Shelly.

"When I was employed at the Zuber Lumber company, we lived in—I guess you'd call it Decatur—we had bought a little three-bedroom house that was probably built in the '50s for $9,000 if I remember right.

"I had a Volkswagen when Shelly was born, but it was tore up. When Angela was having hard labor pains a month early, I ran next door and borrowed their old car to get her to the hospital in a hurry, like Shelly always is—she always wants to be fast! We got there about 12:00, and she was born about ten minutes later. That was a close one, girl."

The fond memories Floyd and Angela shared as we sat around the dining room table for this storytelling session showed the joy they shared of precious memories as a family together over the years. Floyd recalls a doctor's visit Angela had with their second pregnancy.

Floyd asked Angela, "Remember when you went to the doctor, and he was punching you on the belly? What did he tell you?"

Angela replied, "This was our second baby. We hadn't got that first one paid for. So, we went to another and he was wanting his money. As he was poking me on the stomach, saying he was not going to deliver that baby 'til he was paid, I just said okay. And then I called Floyd crying from a payphone across the street, and I told him what the doctor said. It had him upset too. The doctor apparently hadn't realized how young we were and how hard we were trying."

"I borrowed the money to pay for that baby at Zuber Lumber Company," Floyd added. "I was working there, and I paid them back $10 a week until our $300 doctor bill was paid off. Isn't that not correct, Miss Angela?"

Angela responded, "Yes. Then I went back to my other doctor. He said he would never be worried about his money, and I'd better not go anywhere else for the rest of my births. Then, on one of my visits, when I was expecting my fourth child, he called Floyd back there with me and said he would need to explain to us how this was all coming about, and he was cutting up with us really big. He acted like he was really getting all over Floyd."

Floyd and Angela on Gatlinburg SkyLift in the mid-'70s

"I knew it had to have been my fault!" Floyd teased.

The laughter Floyd and Angela exchanged as they shared this and many other stories only brought to light the depth of their love for each other and the experiences of life over the years that had drawn them close.

HOUSE FLIP

Floyd has always been good at finding ways to make money. He seemed to be dreaming, scheming, planning, and thinking of ways to turn a dime into a dollar. Floyd took to house flipping before it was trendy. Floyd always had a project going. One such major project he took on was an old triplex house on Moreland Avenue in Atlanta between 1972 and 1973.

Floyd explained, "A friend, Fletcher Magby, gave me a lead on a bank repo house on Moreland Ave. in Atlanta that could be picked for $15,000. So, I went to look it over. There had been several others who looked at it and thought it was a worthless project, but I jumped on the opportunity."

Floyd now found himself for the next eight to ten months working his day job of 8 to 5 then driving into Atlanta to work on this massive project until 11 p.m., drive back to Douglasville for a quick dinner of beans and cornbread, get to bed only to get up and do the same hard routine day in and day out until the project was complete.

"That seemingly worthless project in the beginning that no one else saw the value in netted me a dandy little profit somewhere in the neighborhood of $10,000. At that time, that was good money." Hard work, long hours, and juggling two or three jobs at once was the only work ethic Floyd knew. He developed this ethic early on, and it has brought him many great rewards.

FAMILY VACATIONS

Floyd and Angela look fondly over the family stories gathered over the years. Floyd recalls one such story from a vacation trip.

"We had gone down to Fernandina Beach for a vacation. It was when Calvin was about four years old. I had a Plymouth with a loud muffler because it needed some work on it. Well, about 11 p.m., after we had all gone to bed, I heard our car right outside our window start up. I knew it was ours because I heard that loud muffler clanging and then *pow, pow*. It sounded like gunshots. I jumped up and ran out the door in just my underwear, and sure enough, there was a guy behind the wheel of my car trying to steal it.

"I ran back in the room, threw on my pants, and ran back out the door to chase the guy down. I didn't know if he had a gun or not. I saw his head bobbing up and down in the ditch across the street as he was running, so I chased him down and tackled him to the ground.

"The police showed up quickly 'cause Angela had called them. That was a scary thing that I just jumped up and did. Didn't really think about it; I just knew somebody wasn't gonna take my car.

"Angela was pretty upset. She said, 'You could have been hurt.' But, I was okay."

The beach seemed to be a favorite vacation destination for the family over the years. While they couldn't afford the most luxurious hotels, and sometimes not even a room, they hold their memories of those times quite close.

"Angela and I took the kids in our Volkswagen on one trip. We didn't have enough money to buy a motel room that time in Panama City. We loaded up three of the kids and headed out real early in the morning. Got to Panama City about 8:00 in the morning, that Saturday morning. We had enough money to get a room for Saturday night, but we slept in the back of the Volkswagen. I don't know if anybody had ever tried sleeping in a Volkswagen with three kids, but we survived. I was stiff for a couple of days. But having two babies, a little one, and two adults in a Volkswagen to sleep was crazy. We had two laying on the seat, one laying over into the back of the backseat, but some good memories of the whole family on that trip.

"There was a guy, John Crawford, that I called on him when I was a manufacturer's rep at Georgia Flush Door. He had bought a little cottage down there off of the main drag in Panama City. For about ten years, he let us go down there for nothing. So, he was a very fine fellow. He died with Lou Gehrig's Disease several years ago. I thought a lot of John.

"So, we enjoyed spending beach time down there for years. In 1987, I ended up buying a duplex in Panama that the family has enjoyed for a long time now. Darcy still remembers us being in Panama City and that Volkswagen trip. She says she never will forget about what we ate for breakfast that morning. I went somewhere and picked up some donuts—sugar-coated doughnuts—and a chocolate milk, and she thought that's the best-tasting stuff she'd ever had. We sat on the beach looking at the ocean and had sugar-coated donuts with chocolate milk for breakfast. Good memories!"

COLONIAL TRAIL HOUSE

In the mid '70s, just after Floyd's transition from Georgia Flush into traveling as an independent manufacturer rep, the family moved into what the four kids thought was a mansion.

Floyd describes the experience.

"The brick house on County Line and Colonial Trail . . . I think we paid $27,000 for it. We got the down payment from Angela's inheritance. It was a big step up for us, and our kids thought we were rich then."

Angela added, "We really never discussed starving or not having rent money or nothing in front of the kids."

Floyd said, "But when we bought that brick house, they assumed we was really in the chips!"

Floyd working on Colonial Trail house additions

The purchase of the house was during some difficult financial times for Floyd and Angela and a lot of business transitions for Floyd. He was in the beginning stages of stepping out on his own and his new junk salvage business was just getting started as well.

"After we were there probably a year, I added on to it. I had always had a small bedroom. That Lake Monroe house bedroom was 8' x 10', and I was always hitting my knees when I got up in the morning to go to work. So, I added on a two-story—a big bedroom about 24' x 24'—and a big den with a fireplace and concrete floor with a dance floor where the kids used to dance. And we had some good times there. We all danced.

"I done most of the work on it myself. We framed it up and found a steel beam in the junkyard and used it. So, I had one big room downstairs, but we had some good get-togethers down there. It turned out to be a nice place."

"We all loved to dance," Angela reminisced. "Well, it relieves a lot of tension. Floyd's a good dancer too."

Enjoying octagon dance floor at family birthday event

CONVENTION DAYS

During Floyd's time with Georgia Flush Door and his time as an independent rep, he and Angela got to experience trade conventions and travel.

"After I'd been at Georgia Flush for a couple of years and learned the business, Walt trusted me more to make decisions, and that's when I started traveling to the West Coast and we started going to conventions. I know we had conventions in New York one time, Washington, DC, San Francisco, Epcot Center in Florida, Bahamas, Jamaica. It was an annual event and a pretty good size. The National Sash and Door Jobbers Association were in the millwork business and sponsored it."

"We had one National Sash Door convention in Atlanta where the manufacturers set up their displays—types of doors and windows—anything to do with the building industry. Georgia Flush Door was a member, and Angela and I got to go."

Angela said, "We made lifetime friends. You can see they took their dress pretty serious. Their dresses cost over $500, and mine cost $14.99! My sister worked at Zayres; she got it for me.

Convention days

"We've traveled the world. We've both said Switzerland was one of the most beautiful places we had ever stayed. We went to Vienna, and we saw the whole Vienna boys choir in the big huge church. We've been to some fantastic places, and there wasn't a dry eye in that place that night when the Vienna Boys Choir performed. Some of their churches had hand paintings on the churches that were built in 1200 BC, and they are most breathtaking. They're 1,300 feet high, and it amazed me how they constructed them.

"In Switzerland, I remember we rode three different trams up the hills. It was like 80 degrees at the bottom and freezing on the top. You got on three different rides that look like they might kill you! Over and through those steep mountains . . . we also rode the Orient Express train. That was one of the most thrilling things I've ever done, riding the Orient Express. We still have our passports.

"This one place we were, this man kept on flirting with me and trying talk to me. He just kept on saying, 'Give me your phone number.' Then I said, 'My husband is just right there. He'll be up here in a few minutes.' And he just kept on. There was a lady with him, and she said, 'Leave her alone.' And the little fella on the bar said, 'Yeah, it's time for you to calm it down.' About that time, I said, 'Here comes my husband.' He looked down and said, 'Please tell me that's not your husband.' I said, 'Yes, it is.' He said, 'Oh, my gosh, I'm losing my job, I know.'

"He knew Floyd knew him, but I didn't know who he was. So, Floyd walking up scared him to death! I did tell Floyd later. I could have embarrassed him to death, but I didn't."

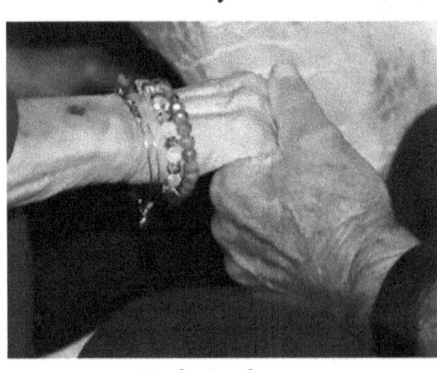
Enduring love

Floyd and Angela laughed about that story. Their expressions and stories made it clear that these convention days were incredibly rewarding for them.

"We got to travel to places we would have never had the opportunity if it hadn't been for those convention days!" Floyd fondly recalled.

CHAPTER 13

LOVE FOR A FATHER

What better testimony exists than the words of family—those who have witnessed you through the good, the bad, the ugly, the stress, the victories, the joyful moments, the sad times, and who have stood by you through both disappointments and successes?

This Floyd C. Davis family is one incredible family. They have endured more than their share of life experiences. Ranging from heartache to mountaintop victories over the last several decades, they have shown mercy, unending grace, tough love and forgiveness, fortitude and strength, deep patience, tenderness, generosity, and kindness. They have lived out and reflected the heart of their father, affectionately known as Daddy and respectfully known as Floyd.

As we were drawing near the end of our story-collecting part of this book project, Mr. Davis asked me if I could gather some stories from his children and his wife, Angela. He insisted the book would not be complete without their input, because "After all, they are my life and the reason I done all this," he humbly said.

DARCY

"He's always stood there for me. Whatever the occasion."

Darcy, the eldest of the Davis children, has had the advantage of watching, learning, and loving her dad the longest. Her recall of countless stories all poured out from her deep-seated love and respect for her daddy. She began sharing her memories with a story from her early days, joyfully recalling, "Daddy's home!"

Daddy's Home!

"My early childhood days, I remember we lived on Lake Monroe Road in Douglasville. It was a dirt road then, and I remember we had a sand pile. I'm not sure if it was for us or if it was for construction or both, but we'd love to play in the dirt, me and Shelly.

"I remember it was when we were really little because we'd be out there in our underwear without a shirt on, and we would be covered up in dirt, and one of us might have peed in our pants, you know, because we were little. We'd be so filthy dirty and then Daddy would pull up in the driveway, and we would just start screaming and running towards him, yelling, 'Daddy's home, Daddy's home!' No matter how dirty we were, he picked us up and hugged us and made it fun.

"We were always delighted to see him, and he was always delighted to see us!"

The Playhouse

"In the backyard at the Lake Monroe house, Daddy had built us a playhouse with leftover wood they used as bracing in the boxcars from when he worked at Georgia Flush Doors. We had an area in the yard that had four or five trees. It was like a natural, shaded space, and they put up a swing. The playhouse was out there too; it had two windows and a porch. We loved it. We would play in it every day. I remember playing bank, house, post office—whatever our imagination could think of. It had a real door, and we loved it, and it was special because our daddy had made it!"

Our Little Pony

"Every little girl wants a little pony and Daddy got us one. We loved it and thought it was the grandest thing ever. I don't know where it was kept. But that little pony beat the hell out of Daddy. It was all the time escaping. Apparently, it didn't like him, you know? Everybody liked Daddy, but this little pony sure didn't! I don't know, but he can tell it better because we were too young to know all the hell he went through with 'our little pony.' I don't remember how long we had it, but it was a Shetland pony."

Beach Trips

"Our family grew up always going to the beach. I'm sure there were years we didn't, but it seemed like we went every year. I remember when I was really little—so little that in the Volkswagen on the passenger side, I could lie down and my feet propped up on the back of the front seat—I could get my whole body on the seat, and I slept that way. So, I wasn't very big. I didn't think anything about sleeping in a car. I'm a little kid. I don't care. Nobody complained about it. That's just what we did. We woke up, and I was at the beach. I never ever thought about how we slept in a car.

"I remember we would drive down and park along the beachfront. I remember waking up parked just off the side of the road at the beach. Daddy would go get chocolate milk and white doughnuts for our breakfast, and when you're a little kid, and there's the ocean, and you've got a cup of chocolate milk in one hand and a white doughnut in the other one, you're in heaven. At that age, you don't know anything any happier than the white donut, chocolate milk!

"We would just stay like two nights, and that one night, would be there along the beach. And then, they would get a motel for the other night, and then we would go back home. I don't remember details about it except that I was so happy. Such a simple life!"

Birthday Flowers

Darcy's 14th birthday flowers

"Daddy and Mama always tried to make our birthdays seem very special. I mean for all of us. A lot of times, one of the grandmothers would make a cake, and cousins and family would come over. It was always really special.

"I remember when I turned fourteen, that seemed really like a big age. I thought it was. I thought I was grown at five, but I really thought I was grown at fourteen. Daddy came in with a dozen roses. I remember him coming in at my birthday dinner at home with those flowers. He did it for each one of us girls, and then I'm not sure what they did for Calvin, but I know something special. It made me feel special. I just felt really grateful."

"After they did the flowers, then they would take each one of us, by ourselves—and this was big—to Steak and Ale near Cumberland. Daddy said, 'I want you to know how to act; I want you to be familiar with nice restaurants, how to act, how to order, and how to be. So, I want you to see this and experience it.' And you know, to me, Steak and Ale is like the best restaurant ever." Darcy hesitated. "Okay, was it really? Or was it the way they talked about it on the way over there.... 'You're gonna love this!' They have the best salad bars. Really, before salad bars were a thing, I think they had a little one, and everything was so fresh. Both of them together, Mama and Daddy, made simple things very special. I think through their enjoyment of life, by how they enjoyed a nice dinner—they noticed and appreciated a good server, a good piece of meat and a nice location—I learned to appreciate simple things.

"They also enjoyed a nice spaghetti dinner at our home. I mean, until I was like way older, I thought spaghetti dinner was like a steak dinner because my mother always made a salad, and everybody had a salad bowl. She always made a spread, and the table always looked wonderful. Having spaghetti usually meant company was coming. We had garlic butter on the bread. We were delighted with even simple cornbread and milk because they made our dinners special no matter what we were having. I feel like I have a joy for life, that I enjoy ordinary things, simple things because they showed me how to enjoy them. I also enjoy nice things, but I can do without them. I like that they gave me an appreciation of nice things but to also celebrate the day—whatever this day is, whether a birthday or whatever, look forward to it, make it special.

"That's the way they lived. They still do."

Easter Guard Duty

"At Easter, no matter how much money they did or did not have, we dressed in patent leather shoes, lacy socks, gorgeous dresses, hats, gloves, and sometimes a pocketbook too.

Darcy and Shelly in their Easter dresses

"Daddy's job on Easter, as Mama got us ready, was to guard us because we were so young, you know, we were so close in age, that we were liable to get really nasty really quick because we lived out on a dirt road. I'll never forget Mama getting us all ready, one by one, and you knew you immediately reported to Daddy. He made sure nobody got dirty or nasty! Daddy had the Easter guard duty over us four little ones!

"I don't remember if they had anything nice for Easter, but I remember we did. Easter was always very celebrated. That was a big deal for them."

Writing on the Wall

"We were in the Lake Monroe house Mama and Daddy had put a lot of work into. The walls had been freshly painted in the house, and it was very nice. It was a wonderful time, and my mother was happy.

"THEN, she found where people had written on the wall! Her freshly painted walls. Tiny people!

"Well, she was furious because they both put a lot of work into this, and they both worked really hard on our house. She was really beside herself. She figured out who did it, and it was me and Calvin because of the height of the writing.

"Now usually if you were in trouble with her, you got in trouble BY her. Well, this time she told Daddy, 'Would you please take them both in there and give them a spanking? I'm so mad at them right now.' She was so upset.

"Daddy marched us into the bedroom sounding very gruff. 'Get in here! Oh, no, you don't do that to Mama, to us; we work hard on this house!' He gave us a pretty strong talking to, a lecture. Then he said, 'Look, I'm gonna hit the bed, but if you don't start crying so your mama knows you got a spanking and then promise her you will never write on that wall again, we'll have to come back in here, and it won't be pretty. So me and Calvin, we cried, and he beat the bed, and we cried and acted like we were killed and swore never to do that again. We were so grateful to Daddy! We never did write on the wall again!

"We didn't tell her for a long time. This was at the Lake Monroe house. We were probably six and three or seven and four. I was like three years older than Calvin."

Daddy Gets to Have All the Fun

"My father was always using a butane torch because our pipes would freeze and the pipes that froze were lead pipes. So, if the pipes froze or burst, he would get out that butane torch and go *play* up under the house with a torch, and I wanted to *play* with that torch. I couldn't touch it; they wouldn't let me touch it. I was a little kid.

"I was secretly jealous of him doing that. Every time, he'd say, 'Let me get my blue flame torch!' and it just fascinated me. So, I was all the time watching him get to play with these cool things. It came to a head when we were coming back from my grandmother's or my aunt's in Atlanta one night in a huge snowstorm. I was a little kid; we were in the Volkswagen. There was snow, and we got halfway down the hill, and we got stuck in the snow.

"I'm in the backseat asleep, and I wake up and I say, 'Wow look at this snow!' And I asked Mama, 'Where's Daddy?' She said, 'He's out there trying to dig us out of this snow because we gotta get home.' Remember my secret jealousy? My response was, 'He always gets to have all the fun!' So they laughed at me for years because deep within, I never meant for that to come out. I was very jealous of the butane torch and now the snow, which is another example of him always having all the fun!

"It was so funny over the years. They're like, 'Yeah, he's out having some more fun!'"

Learning Respect

"Mama and Daddy had a disagreement. He was sitting on the couch with his arms folded looking really grumpy. Mama was in the kitchen washing dishes. Well, I had got in trouble with my mama for something. I don't remember what. I pranced over to him and sat down on the couch, just like he did. I let out a big huff, folded my arms, and I said, 'I'm mad at her, too.'

"He jumped up and pulled me up too and got me by the arm. He said, 'Hey, don't you ever come tell me anything like that about your mother. She is a wonderful mother. She loves you. She loves all of us, and she does a great job. Don't you ever disrespect her.' And, you know, I was shocked because I was on his side. My daddy, in that moment, taught me something about respect, and that is one thing—my daddy and my mama always taught me respect. I think it's a gift that they both taught respect for each other and others.

"No matter how much Daddy worked, or what he was doing, or where he was going, she told us, 'Your daddy is doing this so that we can do this. He's doing this for us. So, what we're going to do is we're going to . . .' and she would fill in the blank. 'We're going to look after him when he gets home.' He did work a lot, and he was gone a lot, but he was also there when we were younger working at home too. He was always making an effort.

"I remember even one Easter all of us dressed up and we had waited on him to finish getting the car fixed. He was always 'having all the fun,' playing mechanic or whatever was needed."

I Could Figure It Out

"Most of my high school afternoons were spent at the shops Daddy had in Douglasville, BML and FDS. I remember doing *Sentinel* newspaper ads when I was fifteen or sixteen. Daddy would say he needed one. I would take a look through literature, do a mockup, and take it up to the *Sentinel* with the pictures. Back then, you had to do your own mockup, glue the pictures on the layout—you had to do the entire ad yourself.

"I did the ads and then up at the store, the one on Bankhead, he would tell me and Shelly to make signs and price everything. We didn't know a lot of the time what they were actually for, but we learned by reading the literature. That's what I tell my people even today. We did merchandising/marketing, and I didn't know that it was merchandising. He just threw us off the deep end.

"I asked him when I was in my 40s, because he and my mama both would just assume that I—we—could do whatever, so I asked him, 'Why did you think I could do so much?' He said, 'Well, I didn't know. I didn't know if you could or not, but I would ask you to do something, and if you would do it, that was great.' He said, 'So I just kept asking you to do more stuff, and you did it.' So he was just thinking that I could figure out different things; I figured them out. Sometimes it was maybe not the greatest results, but it taught me that I could figure out a lot of things if I would just try.

"I heard Daddy say, 'I've just never believed there wasn't anything I couldn't do. I may have to do it again,' or, 'I may have to get somebody to help, but just never thought I couldn't do it.' He taught us that great quality too.

"I thought everybody could drive a forklift, everybody could do a newspaper ad, and everybody kind of knew how business ran. Daddy didn't sit me down and say, 'This is how the business is run.' We saw it, and we jumped in to help whenever they said, 'Do this; do that. Try this; try that. Whatever it took."

Irreplaceable

"I don't remember exactly how old I was; it was either late teens or early twenties. Daddy was doing something; he was changing something—something pretty big—and he must have seen doubt in my face. I mean, because at that time, I knew more than him because, you know, I was the ripe old age of either eighteen or nineteen. He said, 'You don't think that'll work, do you?' I said—I didn't want to be mean—but I said, 'You know, it might, I don't know.'

"I didn't give him any support. I said, 'I don't know.' We went on talking about some other stuff. He came to the realization that I thought that I was irreplaceable, and that's exactly what I thought after my five years on the job.

"Well, he let me go that day! He told me that everybody, believe it or not, is replaceable, and that the graveyard was full of people that believed just like I did—that they were irreplaceable—but that they were [replaceable], and that I needed to think about that. And I did. That was such a humbling experience. He did not humiliate me. He did not make fun of me. I imagined it was kind of funny on his end, except it was also probably pretty aggravating. You don't really have time for people with that big of an ego. It's just like, 'Oh, God, here we go, people that think they are irreplaceable.' So I wasn't there for like a couple of weeks or a month or so. I think I was on administrative leave. He hired me back. It was good for me to learn that lesson. I never had another job with him or anybody else where I thought I was irreplaceable. It made me a better employee and made me a better person. I don't think I'm irreplaceable in my life. I don't think I'm not replaceable. It just means I'm aware that I need to be humble and do what I need to do. It was a hard lesson to learn, one my daddy gently, firmly taught me!'"

Respect for Other Cultures

"Daddy and Mama always wanted us to be open to other cultures and to see what other people did without judgment. Daddy had a Hispanic friend, George. I remember we went to a celebration they were having. Mama and Daddy sat us down and said, 'We're going to George's family celebration.' They said, 'They eat differently than we do, and you're not to go in there and go, "Eww!" or say anything bad. You go in, and you get a little bit of food to try. We're not better than them. This is a new culture, and it's very exciting to know what other people do.'

"That's how we looked at other people, other cultures—no matter what they were, it was exciting. It may be different, but the only way you're going to find out is if you go with an open mind and be willing to take a taste of something different.

"I remember seeing green rice there, and I was like 'Green rice, whoa!' I don't remember anything else about the food except that green rice, which I still don't know what that was. I don't remember if I liked it, but the lesson for me was later on to meet different people from different cultures. I find them fascinating. I usually look for something that I can take with me out of it, a new seasoning, a new way to approach food or life. Observe their way, their mannerisms, or the way their culture is. It's not something to be afraid of. I've never been afraid of somebody being different than me. My mama and my daddy taught me that. Daddy always stressed the importance to treat all people—Black, White, rich, poor, neighbor, or stranger—with the same respect."

The Fun Side

"I know my father's work ethic. He taught it to us. I think there's another side of Daddy that not many see or know. We have always danced together and had fun as a family.

"When we lived on Lake Monroe and were little kids, we were always putting on shows for each other. I remember one song, which Calvin sang best, was, 'Crying Time Again.' You know, 'It's crying time again. You're gonna leave me.' I'll never forget that song because we would do a whole show on 'Crying Time.' We had a console stereo that looked like a dresser with a TV in it, and it was a big deal. We saw the walk on the moon on that TV. It also had a record player and a radio. We would dance in this big space Daddy built onto the house. We would dance to 'Jeremiah Was a Bullfrog,' Creedence Clearwater Revival, Conway Twitty—all the old country songs. We all still dance to this day! My family is very silly. We can cut up when we get together sometimes and act outright silly!

"I was the first one to date. I remember the first time I went out on a date. Everybody was watching me on my first date. Everybody knew when he was coming. They all had gathered in the kitchenette; it was small. When you walked in the back door in the kitchen, the kitchen table was right there on the left. This night, it was full of people—all my family—because I had a date.

"Mama and Daddy were in the kitchen too. So, when my date pulls up and gets out of the car, and I peek out the window, I am very nervous. Well, Daddy messes up his hair, buttons his shirt crazy, and starts acting like there's something wrong with him and being real spastic. The whole bunch of them start laughing and carrying on while I turned fourteen shades of red, and I can't really breathe, and I can hardly speak. It's my first date.

"My date knocks on the door and Mama goes to answer it. Daddy whips back around all fixed back to his normal self while everybody is still laughing. I'm about ready to pass out, and the whole family is laughing right into the face of this poor young man that was probably as nervous as me. My face turns one hundred colors of red, and I just want to run back upstairs! Daddy did that more than once, you know! There's a lot of other silly things we've done over the years. I think having that dance floor and the laughter and kidding was a gift of joy.

"Daddy and Mama talked about dancing and singing together. We were always singing. I think it's how we survived because no matter what, all of us were ready to get up and go dance. I remember Calvin and all of us all going out to eat, and there would be a band. Half the time our dates didn't dance so Calvin, my sweet brother, and Daddy, would. Calvin would say, 'Okay, I'm not dancing ten songs in a row. You can't make me!'

Darcy with her daddy, Floyd

"I'm glad that as much as we worked, we would celebrate too. Daddy threw a big cookout and had somebody come grill, and everybody brought their kids, and we had watermelon and just had good ole fashion fun. He and my mother enjoyed life and liked people."

Bouncing Back From Devastating Blows

"Over the years, our family has not only faced a lot of victories and successes but also more devastating blows that would have ripped most families apart. Through each one, Daddy and Mama's constant love for all of us—children, grandchildren, and extended family—has held us together. They have truly taught us no matter what, you love, you forgive! Period. They taught us you are loved, and you are forgiven. Period!

"Our family is also big huggers, and I can tell you personally those hugs and kisses over the years have carried me through some very hard, dark times. One thing I know about my daddy—he loves me no matter what!

SHELLY

"He never fussed at us; he always let us learn."

Born just fourteen months after her big sister, Shelly was never too far behind Darcy. They have always shared a closeness of heart, possibly due to being so close in age. Floyd and Angela both have said, "Shelly was always in a hurry, trying to rush things. Maybe because she was keeping pace with her older sister or maybe it has been her big love for life that was always pushing her forward."

Shelly began her story time with a big bang!

Trash Burning

"One thing I remember as kids when we lived on Lake Monroe, Daddy had our trash in the backyard in a burn pile. We would get so excited when it was burn time. We would run down there when he would burn, and that was like a simple fun thing, not just burning the trash but all of us kids waiting for aerosol cans to explode! We were waiting on the big bangs!

"It was exciting for us. It was fun, and that was the highlight of the week for us little ones, getting to blow up aerosol cans in the fire!"

Playhouse

Like Darcy, Shelly has particularly fond memories of the playhouse her daddy built for her and her siblings. "It had two little windows and a big, real door," she said. "He was trying to make it special for us, so he put 'Davis' on it, but the Davis sign was on the inside of the door instead of the outside of the door! We didn't really care but looking back, it's kinda funny. I guess we were always reminded we were the Davises every time we went out of that playhouse. We played house, played like it was our bank, and used the windows for the bank teller window and all kinds of stuff. That playhouse allowed us some good play time and for our imaginations to go wild. We really thought we were bankers."

Home From Work

"I remember when he would come home. That was the highlight of our day! We were all ecstatic and glad to see him and he would come in, get us all on the floor on most days, and just tickle us—just the simple way he greeted us by playing and giggling. I think it helped him unwind from his busy days, and I know for us kids, we loved it.

"Thinking back about those times, he always smelt like wood. To this day, I still love the smell of wood on Dad. Sometimes when I smell wood, I flash back to when I was younger.

"Daddy would come in, and we'd always have family dinner together, and now it might be potatoes or beans or just anything, but we had dinner together as a family. We didn't really know it then, but he was so tired, he would lie down on the couch just to rest, and we would crawl all over him, make all kinds of noise. He would be so tired, he slept right through it. He never budged. He always came home no matter how hard he'd been working and had time with us kids!

"At our Lake Monroe house, there was a hill to the left of it, and when we were little riding our bicycles, it seemed like a huge hill. I've since rode back by as a grown up; it's like, oh my goodness, it's just a little hill!

"Daddy bought a lot that had been dug out to build a house on but they didn't build, so some of our best times were playing in that vacant lot. We would go there and play for hours. We would rake up pine straw for walls and play house. We had the biggest time just playing in that graded out lot and the red Georgia clay.

"We played hard while he was gone to work. So, we would just get all covered in dirt—Georgia red clay dirt! We would take baths, and every once in a while, Daddy would give us a bath. He would line up me, Calvin, and Darcy in the bathtub, and he would wash our heads. It seemed like our heads was the dirtiest with red dirt, but he would wash us with Comet to get us clean. He scrubbed our elbows, knees, and feet. We would just be so nasty.

"To this day he hasn't denied washing us with Comet!"

Dropped Potatoes

"One day, we were in the kitchen with Mama helping. She let us help her a lot. We had potatoes or beans often; we didn't have meat hardly ever, and we always had biscuits. One day, I was gonna help her. I just want to cry now talking about it, but I was taking the big pot of potatoes to the table, and I dropped them! Mama started crying, and I started crying. It was awful, an accident, but I felt terrible!

"One reason I think mom started crying was because that was all we had for supper and she didn't have time to cook beans. So, it upset her a lot.

"I think we just got them up off the floor and had them for dinner anyway. It was hard times; we were poor but we didn't know we were poor. We thought the people on the street in the block house was poor. We didn't realize that we had hard times because Mama and Daddy, they never talked about money or troubles, so we didn't know."

"Play-Doh"

"When Mama would have potatoes or beans or whatever we had every day, she made homemade biscuits. Whatever dough she had left over, she would take turns giving that extra dough to the different girls. I know for me, I would just take that dough and sit outside and pretend to make biscuits. It was like a highlight and sweet time. It was kind of like a treat if it was your day to get the dough to play with. It was like Play-Doh from the biscuits.

"She did have a wooden bowl when she made biscuits—the old-timey way—and she made them all the time. I still can't make a good homemade biscuit."

Beach Trips

"I remember every year we got to go to John Crawford's beach house. He and Daddy were good friends, and he let us stay there for free. We were so excited that we would go down before we could even get in the house, drive down early and sleep the rest of the night into the morning on the beach. I remember when we woke up, Daddy would always go get us white sugar-coated doughnuts and chocolate milk. The beach house was next to the FunTime Arcade. They made sure every year we got to go down to that little arcade. We didn't get to eat out a lot or do extras but it was just good fun times at the beach with the family.

"I think that's one reason our whole big family now enjoys the beach so much. Mama and Daddy made it special when we were young and growing up."

Shelly dancing with her dad

Mema Irving

"Here's some things that I remember about Mema Irving, Daddy's mama: she worked very hard, and, buddy, you got up, you made up your bed when you came to her house. She would wrap pecans for Christmas. She loved to bake. She would make all kinds of just homemade decorations. She kept her house neat and clean; I guess that's why I don't like mine messy in all that disarray. She would always have that house cleaned up. And if you spent the night, she would wake you up at night to pee in a cup to keep us from wetting the bed!

Matching outfits Mema handmade for Darcy and Shelly

"Mema Irvin, now, I guess looking back, I don't know how she had the time to do all she did. She would always cut our hair. Some of my pictures of my bangs I didn't realize until now, they were only half-inch long across the top, which is funny to laugh at now. She didn't get to come a whole lot, so when she did, she just would take advantage and do all she could. She would come visit, and she would also bring us dinner. She had this stackable with five aluminum pans, and the lid popped up. She would bring the whole dinner to us: chicken, corn, beans, and usually a lot of vegetables that she grew herself in her garden.

"I remember at Easter, or if we had something special at school, she would make new outfits for us. She did make me, Tonya, and Darcy nice matching Easter outfits.

"The first time we ate out was with Mema and Granddaddy. We didn't eat out much when I was growing up. We might go to Dairy Queen and get an ice cream cone. I remember we'd go to their house, and they would run to Burger King and get us Whoppers. We would have the little Whopper crowns; we thought we were something then! She did have a love for flowers and kept her house clean, and she baked, and just did about everything she could to help us."

Learning Responsibility

"Darcy and I both worked at the door shop, and I was leaving school in the eleventh and twelfth grade at noon as part of the work program. I was working part-time a little bit, and Darcy was working. I was learning how to do the receivables and payables. It was just Daddy and us, and then Mama would help some with payroll and stuff. That kept things going at first.

"We were there all day long. We still have the original ledger book that shows our sales from when he first started. When Darcy left for college, I feel like Daddy just kind of threw me in there to sink or swim! I was working out there by myself, and I didn't really have help. Daddy was down there at the BML place on Duralee Lane not too far away. And I was at the one across from Wickes on Highway 78. Occasionally we did have some older gentleman that would help a few days a week, but on Saturdays, and a lot of the time, you were on your own and just kind of finding your own way or trying to call Daddy or just trying to figure things out.

"Looking back, I feel like that did teach us a lot of responsibility. Daddy wasn't a hover parent. So, you just knew this needs to be done. He would guide us a little bit, and then we would just do the best we could. We made mistakes. We might have sold stuff too cheap, but he felt like that's how we learned. It did take a lot of responsibility and hard work. He never fussed at us, he always let us learn."

TONYA

"Daddy has always helped so many people."

Tonya—affectionately known as Baby Girl by Floyd and Angela—will eagerly tell you all about her daddy's big heart. She takes pride not only in the countless people her dad, Floyd, has helped over the years but also honors him through every story she shares.

Her first story is about a neighbor whom Floyd and Angela not only supported financially over the years but whose life left a deep impression on her. She came to realize this later in life, as a mother herself, thanks to her dad's generous heart.

Our Blind Neighbor

"I remember, as a young child, we would go help JC, our blind neighbor. I was always fascinated with him being blind, like the way he ate, and he would listen to TV with us. He would laugh when we laughed, and I was just amazed. I remember going to JC's house. He made mops and brooms. There was a little barn out back where he made them. We went to their house one day, and he wanted to show us how he made the mops. Daddy went and got a light bulb to put in the socket so we could watch him make them because obviously, he didn't need the light. We got to watch him make the mops. That's a really good memory. I remember Daddy helping him. I believe at that time, Daddy and Mama probably didn't have much themselves. We found checks, and they were checks made out to Bell South for JC, and they also paid his electric bills. Daddy always helped him out. That just makes me so proud of my Daddy caring for him, even in our own tough times.

"I remember him being at the house. Mama had told me a funny story that they had taken him to the courthouse for some reason. She said that they were walking down a lot of steps, and she forgot to tell him 'Steps.' They rolled down all these steps, Mama and him. Of course, that was a funny story.

"I just remember being fascinated with JC, and then having a blind daughter myself, it just brought back memories. I realized how much that had an impact on my life. It's good memories of the way Daddy has always helped so many people. I hear stories all the time of the people that my father's helped. Even at work today, people still come in and tell me how much Daddy helped to get their first car or send their child through school or let them get a loan for $500. I just know what I remember most about my father is his giving heart and always blessing others.

"I've always thought how it was funny to experience the blind culture as such a young child, and then for me to find out later in life that my daughter was blind. I feel like I did get to experience some of that to prepare me. I thought about JC often when I found out Tale was blind. So that early experience and exposure to what it was like to be blind did introduce me to how her life would be. I know that he managed his life. I just remember him eating and feeling around for his food, and he survived and was supporting his family. I remember visiting JC a lot and just being fascinated, and that he was a kind man. They were poor, and Daddy always helped them."

Good Christmas

"At Christmas time, I just remember we always had a lot. They would give us bikes and go-karts. I don't know how they did that, and it might not have been so much. Being the youngest, I just don't ever remember not having a good, big Christmas. There's pictures of us at Christmas, and I always thought we had a great Christmas. It was great to me.

"I don't have the same memories like Daddy pushing the Volkswagen. I was too young. It used to bother me that I didn't have the same memories, but Daddy helped me understand being the youngest—he says the best is always saved for last!

"The things I do remember was my daddy and my mama loved us."

Beach Trips

"I do remember always going to Florida. I don't remember all the details about it, but every year we went. We would stay at John Crawford's house. I do remember we were right beside FunLand Arcade. That was a real good memory: arcade, ice cream, and the beach! We have pictures of us on the steps. . . . I remember always having fun, and I just remember that that was one thing they always did with our family was to make sure we went to Panama City every year. We all have really fun memories of those trips."

Family Dinner Time

"I remember Mama fixed dinner every night at the Colonial Trail house. We all would sit down together and eat dinner. That's some really fun memories. We all had our certain spot that we would sit in. I remember Daddy always being there, us six, and a puppy under the table. We always sat down and ate dinner. It was a blessing to sit down and eat dinner with your family, it is so important. That was very important to Mom and Daddy.

"Our conversations, they were happy ones, with much laughing. Each of us would tell about our day, just whatever came to mind in school; sometimes report cards would come up, and I wouldn't be thrilled about that. I just remember it being a pleasant family time and realizing now what an honor to be able to just sit down and have those memories from my childhood."

Working the Family Business

"Each of us had our time working in the family business. In the BML days after Darcy headed off to college, Shelly was up there all the time. She was good at what she did. I started coming up there after school. I'm guessing my age was probably about fourteen. I knew nothing about anything, doors or windows, moulding. I had no clue. I would go up there after school and when customers came in, I would hide in the closet and leave Shelly up there to handle all the customers. I've worked in and out of there all my life, and now I'm at a place at Building Material Liquidation that Dad has allowed me to run it now. And that is a privilege and an honor for him to trust me with such a big responsibility.

"I remember a lot about Floyd Davis Sales. I believe he had a door line at the time, too. There were a lot of us upfront doing bookkeeping, and Mom always did the payroll, of course. I remember working under Shelly most of the time, and she was always good to me. She was sick a lot. They all had a lot of patience with me, but I have really fond memories of working around my family. It's my job now, and I enjoy it."

Platelets for Chrisha

"Daddy has not only loved us kids deeply, but he loves his grandchildren! I remember how he helped his granddaughter, Chrisha.

"Shelly and I actually were pregnant at the same time, me with Casey, and her with Chrisha. I believe when Chrisha was about two, she was diagnosed with leukemia. I remember that Mama was always up at the hospital, and so was Daddy. It was a very hard time for both of them. I remember Daddy going up there all the time and giving Chrisha his platelets. He would go sit for hours and give his blood all the time. Mama and Daddy both were really supportive of Shelly. It was a really hard time in our life.

"We all got through, as they have with other adversities. I do know that Daddy giving his platelets all the time for Chrisha means a lot to Shelly."

Trip to Hanging Dog

"A few years back Daddy took all the grandsons to his beginnings, his heritage in Hanging Dog. I had the privilege to go along and capture some great times, memories, and pictures. There was Davis Creek. It was an amazing trip. Daddy was so proud of that area and sharing all he could about his family heritage. We got to look at the cemetery; it was so old. Just to think, him growing up there, it was a real memorable moment. All the boys got to go—Daniel, Jacob, Jonathan, Calvin, and Casey. It was fun watching him so excited sharing with his grandsons. It was an unforgettable trip, and I'm lucky I got to go and take pictures and be a part of it."

Floyd with his grandsons Kasey, Daniel, Calvin, Jonathan, and Jacob

Work Ethic

"Daddy has always, always been a hard worker. That's what he's always done. He's been successful at it. He has instilled in us kids that you have to work; it doesn't just come to you. You have to go out there and get it.

"I remember him saying more than once to me over the years, you have to take some risk. I believe that's why he's been so successful. He has worked hard all of his life and been willing to take risks. Not foolish risks but put it out there with hard work.

"He's made the comment to me that, 'I'm sorry I wasn't there as much.' I don't remember him not being there. He was there. I don't remember an absent father. I just hear that he traveled a lot, but I don't remember him ever being absent in my life.

"Definitely hard work is his motto, and there's a quote at the shop he posted: 'Every job is a self-portrait of the person who did it. Take pride in your work and respect the work of others.' That's the quote we have hanging today still at Building Material Liquidation. My dad's message of success!"

Mama's Support of Daddy

"Daddy had several different business ventures, and a few times, he was not that successful. I think he said the last time we went out, my mom was like, 'Look, you need to either get it this time, or we need to find you something else to do.' And as the story goes, they had gone out of town for the weekend. I think he was thinking he would have to get another job or do something different when he came back. And when they got back in town, he had a check in the mailbox. It was from when he was repping for companies, and so that started another career, and he ended up being successful that time.

"I do know that Mama had his back each time. Every single thing that he did, she was there, and she would support him. Even when he did travel a lot and he had a lot to do, she stayed home and looked after us. I'm sure there were some sacrifices with her that she gladly did. You know, my mom, she was a great mom, and of course, my daddy was a great daddy.

"A funny story about his traveling days: I do remember when he was busy with his repping and traveling, he was getting a lot of business calls. Me and Calvin, we were kind of young, and we'd be on the phone all the time with our friends, Calvin with his girlfriends, and Daddy would get business calls, and we would forget to take messages for him.

"So, what Daddy ended up doing was getting me and Calvin our own phone. That way Mama could answer the phone, get business calls and messages, and the phone would ring and not be busy all the time.

"Yes, I do remember my mama would support everything that my daddy did, and long before I was even around."

Reading Draft of Book

Floyd with his daughter Tonya

"I was over at Mom and Dad's recently, helping him one evening, and it was about time for me to go. Daddy had brought in a printed copy of the first six chapters of this book, and he was talking to Mama about it and asked if she had read it. He was showing me the chapters, and we were reading parts of it. Mama was already in the bed, and he came in, sat on the bed with her, and I had it in my hand and I began reading to them. I ended up reading all six chapters out loud to them, which ended up being just a huge blessing and great memories for me. One I will always cherish. It was just a lot of good memories, with some tears from reading parts of it. It was just a good memory made. We would tear up, then we would laugh. That is a memory that I will never ever forget. It was a privilege."

Tonya made sure he knew to let her read the remainder of this book to him.

ANGELA

"Floyd is the kindest man I've ever known."

Angela's love story began when she and Floyd met in their early adult years in the 1950s. She was seventeen and he was twenty-two when they married. For over sixty-three years, they have weathered a remarkable life together. Throughout the years, they have achieved many victories together, accomplished much, and weathered many storms along the way. While the years have blessed Floyd and Angela with many wonderful memories, they have also faced some devastating events that struck their family. One of the most devastating blows to Floyd and his family was the unforeseen passing of Angela during the writing of this book. For sixty-three years, Floyd has shared everything with Angela—his dreams, his aspirations, his failures, his heart, his wealth, and every night, his bed. This season ahead for Mr. Davis—Floyd, Daddy—will be one of his most challenging yet.

The Davis family, however, knows that true strength is found in times of sorrow and adversity by allowing their hearts to come together. He is surrounded by a wonderful legacy of family who loves him each and every day.

Angela, affectionately known as Grangie, shared these thoughts and stories with me just three days before her unexpected passing. The fact that Angela's words were captured at just the right time feels like a miracle, leaving us all to wonder if she sensed her time to pass on to heaven was near.

Her love for Floyd and her family has always beamed from her heart and shone in her angelic smile.

Kind Man

Before her passing, Angela shared many precious memories of her husband.

"Floyd's a man of his word. I don't know anybody that has ever known Floyd that does not know he's a man of his word, because if he says he would do it, it's done! He makes sure to keep promises.

"He is so kind-hearted. You and anyone who knows him has probably seen that. Can you tell me if you've ever seen anyone so kind-hearted, even in the business side as well? Not to just his family, but to all people and strangers?

"He has never, ever asked anybody to do any work for him that he wouldn't do himself.

Floyd and Angela in their early years

He doesn't depend on others to do things that he wouldn't do. He's a strong man—a little independent maybe—but at his core, he's just kind. He's just a different kind of person than most. A good man. A very good man."

His Care for Us

"We—Floyd and me—have talked about how we wanted our home to be from the time that we had children. We were not wanting to be loud and screaming parents. We would always try to keep our cool in front of the kids. We always just said we wanted our home to be full of fun and laughter and joy for the kids. Everything that was ever done by Floyd was to help take care of his children and me. He loves his family."

Our Dancing Days

"One thing Floyd doesn't really let people know is he got the first pouring liquor license in Douglas County! Don't tell him I told you."

One thing that was not a secret was their love for dancing.

"We always loved to dance. Our favorite restaurant was a place called DJs because you could eat dinner there, and they had a band and a dance floor. The guy in the band liked to always sing songs for me that I requested. One night, the owner got up and said over the microphone he thought he was going to have to close the place down because things were running slow, but that Floyd Davis had just bought DJs that night, so they were staying open for business!

"I was shocked! Floyd hadn't told me that he was going to buy the place. We ended up enjoying owning the restaurant for a short while, and that's how Floyd got the first pouring liquor license in Douglas County—to keep DJs up and running."

Miracles

"Our family has had a lot of miracles over the years.

"The first miracle I knew . . . was a drunk driver coming down the road at my grandparents. He run right between me and my sister playing; it was within an inch of both of us on each side. My grandmother came running down the steps, saying that was a pure miracle. I was probably six years old. My sister was little. It was just really, truly a miracle.

"We've faced hardships ever since then, and there have been miracles over and over—my health, we've had wrecks, the kids have had accidents, and we've just seen so many miracles in our life. I just can't believe how many, and I could talk for three or four hours about it. All the miracles.

"We wanted to make sure that we had love and laughter in our home. We wanted to make sure that we tried to help everybody we could possibly help. I think God has blessed us tremendously with our family."

Angels Among Us

"We have had a lot of death; I call them angels among us. Having a big family, there have been more deaths than we wanted. A son, two granddaughters, and a grandson. Then after that, we've had so many wonderful, wonderful friends and family members to pass. Floyd's brother, Mac, and my sister, Frankie. They are angels among us.

"Floyd and I have been blessed over and over and over with the people that God has put in our lives and crossed our paths with. So many wonderful people."

We Made It Through
"I told Floyd just last night, I always said, 'I'm so glad that we made it through all these years.' We really have never talked really ugly to each other. We didn't, we couldn't. I don't know if it's because we got married so young—I was seventeen, he was twenty-two. But we just knew not to talk ugly. He's never called me an ugly word. Now, he probably has behind my back... just kidding.

"I feel so beyond blessed. No matter what's been going on, the kids are being right here helping. I don't have a child or grandchild—anybody in our family—that wouldn't help us. I mean we are blessed with our family. And it's kinda sweet to think it all started with Floyd and me."

MEMORIES OF OUR PRECIOUS CALVIN
In the storytelling collection process of this book, it became clear the voice of Calvin, Floyd's only son, was not present. This section is a mixture of stories told by Floyd, Angela, Darcy, Shelly, Tonya, and Andrea, Calvin's widow. While these stories reflect many joyful memories of Calvin, collecting them was bittersweet. The loss of a son and brother in his early 40s brings a profound and unanswered question: why so young? This section is lovingly dedicated to Calvin.

Darcy started:

"I remember at the Lake Monroe house in Douglasville, one time, us girls and Mama were in the kitchen. We had a kitchen island with a countertop on it. Well, a rat came running through the kitchen and scared all of us girls. Mama, Shelly, and I all jumped up on the counter screaming! We were terrified! Calvin, who was about six or seven, came in there and ran the rat out the door. We were all relieved and started telling Calvin how he

"I remember playing Calvin a song at a party he was having. I made everybody get quiet and played 'Lean on Me,' and at the part where it says, 'Call on me, brother, when you need a hand,' I blasted it. I know that touched him. He gave me his sweet grin and laughed. I loved him so much. He had a happy heart.

Darcy and Calvin

"Calvin and Andrea had been together a while. Andrea came to talk to me. She had a few tears and said she wanted to get married and was concerned that Calvin didn't. I went to talk to him one morning and I started to give my little brother my big sister advice. He tried to interrupt me. I said, 'Please let me finish,' and he sat grinning at me the whole speech and let me finish. Then he left the room and came back to show me her engagement ring. He laughed and laughed at me, as he so often did.

"When Daddy finished the addition on the Colonial Trail house, Calvin got to have the downstairs bedroom. At first, I was a bit jealous—okay, a lot jealous, because after all, I was the oldest. But after our parents said, 'He has waited so long on you girls for the bathroom; it is time he had some space,' I completely understood and realized he had earned that bedroom and space.

"I remember Christmas at Colonial Trail, and my parents were able to give us nice presents. A very fond memory I have is my father being so delighted to be playing racetrack and other boys' games with Calvin. It's a very precious memory. Daddy was so proud of Calvin and loved him dearly."

It was clear that Floyd cherished all the little things that made Calvin unique. "Calvin's nickname was Cowboy. You could find him in his cowboy hat any day!" Darcy said.

Calvin was also quick to lend a helping hand in times of heartache and trouble.

"I had separated my daughter from Tamara's father when she was very young. Calvin and Daddy came to Pelham to help get my stuff. It was a very difficult time for me. Calvin and I were standing outside, and he said, 'I will help you with her.' He said, 'I will be her father figure.' It touched my heart—this skinny, adorable little brother of mine was quite a man. He felt family responsibility like our father. I was so proud of him, and those words were such comfort to me."

Calvin's Grin

Darcy continued to share her fondest memories of Calvin.

"We were all close in age and had different ideas and points of view. Calvin and I would disagree about something and would find out who was right eventually, and Calvin would grin delightedly to correct his older sister. He would say, 'Was I right or was I right?' grinning from ear to ear, and I had to laugh with him. How could you resist that happy, precious heart?

"When Calvin was born, I was so in love with that baby boy. I wanted to help be his mama, too, so I shared my cup of water with this tiny little guy and almost choked my new baby brother!"

Shelly echoed many of Darcy's memories about Calvin but also shared her own unique set of recollections.

"At the Lake Monroe house, it seems like there was always a lot of construction going on. One time, there must have been work happening up on the roof, and the big, tall ladder was left standing propped up against the house. Calvin was about three or four. Mama went outside looking for him and couldn't find him at first. Then she spotted him up on the roof! Mama was horrified and panicking he was going to fall off. So, she very nervously—shaking all over—climbed up the ladder talking real sweet and calm to

Kids gathering Easter eggs

Calvin. They both got safely down the ladder. Calvin was proud of his ladder experience while Mama was a nervous wreck. Calvin was a bit of a risk-taker. Wonder where he got that from?"

Tonya, Floyd's youngest daughter, had this to say:

"When Daddy worked at Georgia Flush Doors, Calvin and I got to go with him on Saturdays sometimes. That place had a big warehouse, like a quarter of a mile long. It was so big they had these scooters the workers would ride to get from end to end. Our highlight was getting to ride the scooters around the warehouse while Daddy did his office work.

"I also remember Daddy getting Calvin and me motorcycles, Kawasaki KD100s. My first ride I ran straight into the building! Calvin and I would ride those motorcycles from sunup to sundown. At the end of our road was a mud field we called clay top. We spent hours on end riding there. It was lots of fun and fond memories. We did have some of our neighbors call the police on us for riding on the subdivision streets! We were just kids having a good time."

Andrea recalls her own special memories of her late husband.

"Calvin and I were married in 1994. We had two children, Angela Sue, named after Calvin's mother, and Calvin Jr., named after Calvin and his dad. Calvin was a hard worker just like his dad. He worked all his career at Building Material Liquidators for Floyd. He worked everything you could there, from sales to deliveries to warehouse and production.

"One special memory I have that meant the world to Calvin was, Floyd would call Calvin every morning about 5:30-6 a.m.

Floyd was very upbeat, saying things like, 'Time to get the day going! The birds are singing! Flowers are blooming! Let's get up and join them!' It was always some happy saying to make you feel good and want to get out of bed. Then Floyd and Calvin would plan the day, their work agenda, everything that needed to be done. Calvin always looked forward to the early morning call from his dad.

"Floyd taught Calvin that hard work paid off. He didn't just give Calvin everything. Calvin had to work hard for his keep just like everyone else. Floyd was a good example in Calvin's life. He taught him the value of a dollar, to be his own self, and always encouraged Calvin, 'Life is what you make it. Go after what you want. Go get it.'

"Floyd's kind spirit and heart were part of who Calvin was. He, just like his dad, always liked helping people. Calvin was also a big family man like Floyd. I know these are qualities Floyd instilled in him over the years.

"Floyd loved sharing his dreams and plans and visions with Calvin, and it meant so much to Calvin to have Floyd's trust."

At this point in the family interview, Floyd chimed in:

"Calvin and I were close, and just like every dad desires to have a son to teach him the family business, that's what I did with Calvin. He was a spunky guy from the beginning. Always full of life and laughter. From jumping in the pool fully dressed on a family beach trip, only to have me fully dressed dive in after him, to climbing up on the house roof when he was about three or four, to his motocross cycling days, to always being the life of the party; Calvin brought our family a lot of joy.

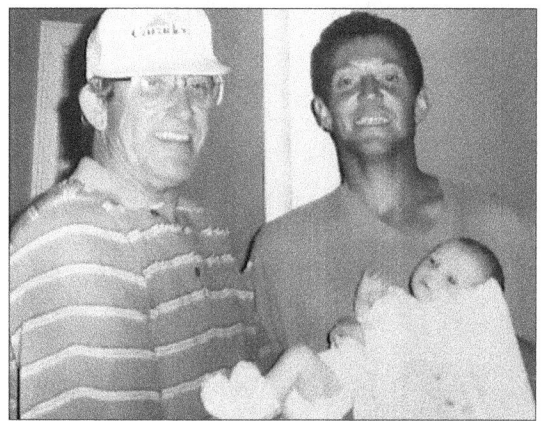

*Three generations of Davises—
Floyd, Calvin, and Calvin, Jr.*

"I don't remember a time when Calvin wasn't some part of the business. He roamed the warehouse as a little guy and worked his way up in the business learning every part of it. He helped me run the Woodstock operation. He worked everything from ordering inventory, to stocking, and sales. We've always been all hands on deck, and he pulled his weight just like the girls did. I think sometimes he felt he needed to handle more just because he was the son.

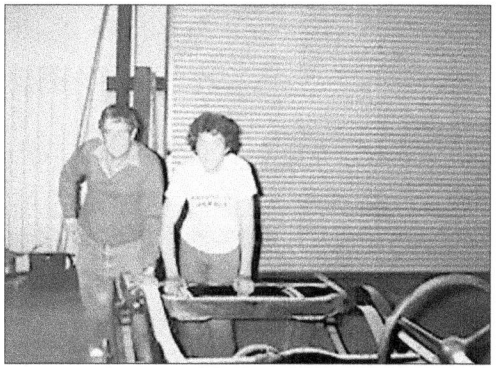

Floyd with his son, Calvin, working in the shop

198 THE MAKING OF A LEGACY

"I know his unexpected passing left a big hole in our family."

As the interview progressed, it became clear that Floyd's true legacy extends far beyond wealth and success—his greatest achievement is his family, a legacy that will endure forever.

The Floyd C. Davis Family

CHAPTER 14

WORDS FROM CRYSTAL

Every story has a chapter you'd rather keep locked away, fearing judgment from others if it were brought into the open. But fear has never directed Floyd's life, nor has the judgment of others.

While writing this book, Floyd approached me with a desire to include a deeply sensitive subject in his life story—one that could reveal a significant weakness—a part of his life that most would be reluctant, embarrassed, or ashamed to share. It was a difficult situation but also one that he felt strongly about including.

Before I go any further, I would like to say that through the years, I have personally witnessed how the entire Davis family has walked through this journey together. I have seen an abundance of forgiveness extended to a husband, a man honoring his wife's rightful place in the aftermath, and the deep love sisters have shown to one another. I have witnessed many accept unanswered questions, yet I've also seen a commitment to taking ownership and a lifelong dedication to resolution.

I have witnessed that weakness can be overcome with the love of family.

The following stories are from Crystal Handley, the daughter that Floyd fathered with another woman at a most vulnerable time in his career.

A NEW FAMILY
Crystal recalled:

"The first time I met the Davis family, we met at the Mansion Restaurant in Carrollton. I was about to turn seventeen. It was a scary and exciting experience. At this dinner, I was introduced to everyone—Darcy, Shelly, Calvin, Tonya, and Angela.

"Over my early years, I had not had the opportunity to know much about my dad. I think my mom was trying to shelter me from what I didn't know or understand. But one day, when I was about twelve, I was in the grocery store with my mom, and I told her I wanted to call and talk to my dad. From that first phone call on, I began to get to know my dad, and for me, I began to start to know what real family is like. It was at this dinner meeting I began to learn and discover my new and additional family.

"I think the biggest lesson I've learned from Daddy over the years when it comes to making big decisions is to always rely on him and talk to him about anything. I remember when I first started working at Tanner in Carrollton, it was a big company that offered pension plans. I remember him asking me, 'So, does Tanner match your pension because a lot of companies, they'll do that as a way, you know, to push employees to save.' Off the top of my head, I start telling him I know all about it, and he jumps in with, 'Well, how much are you putting in?' I told him, and I wasn't putting anything in but like, 1 percent. And his tone went from, like, calm and conversational to stern and unbelief. He says, 'Crystal, that's just throwing away free money; what are you thinking? You have to raise that up to at least to what they match.'

"I will remember that forever because it opened my eyes to the importance of saving and making money. Being young, I didn't really have a clue. I've carried that with me. I work in HR now, and when people come up to me and they ask me about pension, I tell them the same advice my dad gave me—'At least put in what the company matches because if not, you're pretty much throwing away free money'—just like he told me.

"I remember it was his reaction that kicked my butt in gear, and if I would talk to him and ask for advice, or I would be kind of just venting about stuff that I was going through, he would always tell me that there is no utopia. There's not a perfect life. There's no perfect anything. Basically, you're always going to have to work, to put something into everything you do, and he said I should never expect some fairytale ending, in a sense, with life in general. There's always gonna be something you're gonna have to work for and work hard for it. And I guess that general saying kind of resonates with me because in life, we always kind of get bumped down a few notches sometimes, and I just have to remind myself that even though that may be the case, that at the end of the day, there may not be any utopia, but at the same time, that's okay; that's just life."

Even though life wasn't perfect for Crystal and the Davis family, she beamed at her daddy's heart for her and her daughter, Natalie.

"When my daughter Natalie was a baby, I took her to the Wedowee house where Daddy and Angela lived. On this particular visit, we spent the night there. This was like their first opportunity to spend time with Natalie as a baby. I will remember and cherish that visit because they wanted to be a part of our lives, and they wanted us there, and even though it was something so simple, I'll always remember that just because that's not something that you always do as an adult child—go spend the night with your parents. But I was thankful I had an opportunity before I started going back to work when Natalie was young to actually spend time with them and for them to have an opportunity to be around Natalie when she was a baby. And it's not necessarily that any particular thing happened, it's just how during that time with them, with Natalie being that small, and them being there for me, meant a lot to me. And maybe that wasn't like a deep thing, but it was just the support they showed me at that time.

"One incident I don't think any of us will ever forget is when they lived in Wedowee at the lake house. I was in the kitchen with Grangie, and we were, I think, fixing food or something, and Natalie had on those little regular floaties that you blow up. You just put them on their arms to help them afloat, and she goes to jump in the pool—she's gonna show off like tricks or some stuff that she can do. Granddaddy was out there with her, and out of nowhere, one of the floaties started to deflate. Well, she starts to kind of get scared and freaks out. And all we saw is him, out of nowhere, jump in the pool with clothes, phone, keys, everything to save her. And of course, he doesn't know in the moment what all is going on. He just knows she's kind of freaking out.

"That's one memory we both will never forget. How Granddaddy jumped in the pool fully dressed to save Natalie."

Floyd's generosity and tender heart extended far beyond his family.

"Daddy has always had a very giving heart, and I have two stories that touched me deeply. I believe it was probably within the last few years, Daddy had some people working for him that their mother passed away. They didn't have any kind of life insurance or anything, and I was able to find out how Daddy basically helped provide this family with the financial way to bury their mother. Without Daddy helping out, I don't know what this family would have done.

"That's no small feat because it probably cost several thousand dollars, if not more.

"And then there is one story that I'll forever hold very dear to my heart. I call her my sister, Brandy, but not on my dad's side. Dad's always known about her. Brandy is my cousin by blood, but she was raised as my sister on my mom's side. So, my sister has always known about Floyd being my dad.

"She struggled from the time since she was probably in her teens. Her first job she ever had was at a bar at Taco Mac in Douglasville. She has had a bad history with her real parents—drugs, alcohol, you name it. You know that's kind of how she got put in the care of Mom because her parents were never in a position to raise her correctly. I know my dad a few times helped her out. I think she had a busted windshield, and he replaced it. So, you think something small like that is no big deal, but to someone struggling, it means a lot.

"Basically, Brandy struggled with alcoholism for most of her life since the time she was probably eighteen. Well, about three years ago, I don't know what prompted her to do it, but she called my dad. I don't know how she got his number or what happened. She called him bawling her eyes out crying and needed help. My dad contacted Josh, a pastor friend, and he ended up going to my sister's house, and from there, between the two of them—Floyd and Josh—they pretty much helped her start her road of recovery. And since then, she hasn't drank and she's been sober. So, for me, that's a personal thing, because I've experienced her life changing and it all started from her calling my dad.

"So, he would never obviously publicly announce who it is or how he helped, and he would never take the credit. But that started from her making that call and Floyd helping."

Though vague, some of Angela's fondest memories of her daddy involve Calvin.

"I have one precious memory I will always treasure. Calvin and I both share the same birthday, and right before he passed, and honestly a little bit right after I met him and the girls for the first time, Daddy, Angela, Calvin, and I met for a birthday lunch at Waffle House in Douglasville, Fairburn Road. I remember the booth we all sat at. I remember Calvin teasing the waitress and telling her we were twins. I remember everything about that lunch just because it was such a special memory for me because it's one with just the four of us.

I think also because it being the last time seeing Calvin, I remember the laughter, the joy of the moment, Calvin's smile, just his warmth celebrating with me. Being able to share it with Daddy and Angela was, to me, special, because I do not have very many memories of Calvin."

While many children in Crystal's situation might have struggled with feelings of alienation and being an outsider, it was the profound, unwavering love of her family that made all the difference.

"I know the uniqueness of my situation is not common, and maybe one that could destroy a lot of homes. One thing I can say about this situation is I never felt like the left-out child or banished from the family. From the time I was introduced to Darcy, Shelly, Calvin, Tonya, and Angela, not one of them made me feel less than, and that says a lot about their character. My dad has always looked out for me, helped me, supported me, encouraged me, and been there for me. That says a lot about his character and about him as a father.

Floyd with Crystal

"Over the years, I think we all have developed our own relationships with each other, and, overall, I can truly say everyone has accepted me as part of the Davis family. I consider myself very blessed."

EPILOGUE

Floyd C. Davis Quotes and Thoughts

In my final interview with Floyd, he shared a tale about his encounter with some much-needed R&R! While work has always been his first drive, passion, and priority, he did try to make time for leisure and rest.

He shared:

"I did have an R&R investment once. It didn't quite work out as I thought it would. It was a time when all my businesses seemed to be growing, making money, and I think I lost my head a bit and began to think 'I've got it made now!'

"Well, I shopped around and found a big cruiser boat in Panama City Beach, and I bought it. I had it moved up to Knoxville on the Tennessee River. Since I was spending a lot of time up there with the big businesses, I thought it would be great to have it close by to enjoy. So, I rented a covered boat slip at the marina on the river and had it stored there.

"Well, come that year, Knoxville had a record snowstorm come through. About twenty inches of snow fell quickly in the area, and to everyone's surprise, it caused some unexpected damages. I like to tell it as the snowstorm that sunk my boat!

"About 20 inches of snow piled up on the canopy over the boat. It couldn't handle the weight of that much snow and caved in on my boat and sank it in the Tennessee River! I didn't even get a handful of rides in that boat before the snow sank it!

"I paid to have it raised up and brought it over to the Knoxville Door location and parked it. Ended up selling it for $10,000, about 3 percent of what I paid for it. I took a huge loss on that boat!

"I tried to have a little R&R! It don't work for me!"

****

Remember the question posed at the beginning of this book: "Who is Floyd C. Davis?" If you haven't already guessed, here's the answer—drumroll, please....

He is a self-made millionaire!

"It's my nature—if you can't figure it out, find another way to try, or do it yourself."

Floyd C. Davis Quotes and Thoughts

Maybe you're asking why the author wouldn't make this the main theme of the book? Wouldn't that sell millions of books? Perhaps Floyd has already seen, already made his millions. I suppose it was intentionally saved for the end of this book because, in his humble way, Floyd Davis has always wanted to be known for who he is—valued for his character. He has sought to be remembered as an ordinary man with a rich story, one who was born poor-poor. The self-made millionaire happened because, in his own words, "I worked my hiney off."

****

When I asked Floyd what words he would like to leave to encourage his family, friends, and anyone looking to start a business or just live a good life, he said, "I think I've left a lot of words to choose from in this book, you pick something." Given that liberty, I've highlighted several powerful messages that Floyd C. Davis has lived by, with the hope that you, too, will find inspiration and encouragement:

"I have always tried to let my kids, my family, know how much you can do if you put your mind to it. That's one reason I wanted to get this book of stories together. I want future generations, not just my own, to know that some guy from little ole Hanging Dog did the impossible! And you can too, if you work your hiney off! Don't be afraid!

"I can't tell you how many times in life I have had to use that same mindset—you do what you have to do. " His journey is a thread of hard life lessons and remarkable victories woven throughout one big heroic journey:

- Move from Kannapolis, NC: *"I didn't have one red cent in my pocket."*

- Chattanooga sales story: *"Even without a red cent in your pocket, you can still make things happen."*
- Sears and Harbor Plywood story: *"Don't be afraid of hard work, you're gonna need it if you want to succeed."*
- "I learned that the harder you work, the more money you made."
- First full-time job at Harbor Plywood: *"You can always learn from someone who has been there before."*
- "That was learning from somebody who had been in the business a long time."
- Wilson Freight Lines: *"That's where I learned hard work, well before that too, but that was really hard work, working by yourself."*
- "Sometimes you gotta do it all by yourself."
- Expanding BML: *"Don't let 'can't' stop you. Figure it out."*
- "It's my nature—if you can't figure it out, find another way to try, or do it yourself."
- BML—Building our own business: *"There's self-reward when it's all done."*
- "We enjoyed building a business that we could say, 'look what we done.'"
- Beach breakfast: *"Enjoy the small things, sugar coated donuts and chocolate milk by the ocean for breakfast."*
- "We parked on the beach looking at the ocean and had breakfast, sugar coated doughnuts, and chocolate milk. Good memories!"
- Claudia Boarding House: *"Never forget what you didn't have."*

- "I thought I was something else. I had new underwear and a new pair of blue jeans and penny loafers."
- "One thing I have always thought—that I could do whatever I wanted to. Give me a challenge, and I was up for it."
- Sawmill in Wedowee: *"You're the only one who can stop you."*
- Building in Wedowee: *"Be resourceful, and don't be afraid."*
- "I wasn't afraid to tear it down and then relocate it and rebuild it. I couldn't afford to buy a new one."
- Sheetrock business: *"One day you'll look back and say 'I can't make up these things.'"*
- "It was an experience, and that's a true story."
- Biloxi House: *"Success asks for sacrifice."*
- "In 1987, I had a house down in Biloxi, Mississippi, that me and Angela really loved to go to. And I needed some money to get the high-production door machine, so I sold the house in Biloxi."
- YMCA: *"Remember the good."*
- "I remember good thoughts about that time."
- Bruce Almore Sheetrock: *"I always needed a challenge, and I seem to have the ability to look into situations to see if I can make it turn into money."*
- "This was my gift in life."
- Business across from Wickes: *"So being across the street from their entrance, I thought that'll be a heck of a location."*
- "Always look for the best position in life."

- Business Acumen: *"I don't consider myself a guru of how to run a business but I've been fairly successful at it and the reason why, I don't know, except to attribute it to hard work and taking chances and not being afraid to make decisions."*
- Life Accomplishments: *"I have always believed adversity builds one's confidence. I have always believed I could do anything anybody else could."*
- "There ain't no way a boy from Frog Holler should have accomplished as much as I have. But I did!"

Floyd Davis is a simple man with a remarkable range of gifts that will impact generations to come. His journey from humble beginnings to building a thriving empire of businesses is a testament to resilience, vision, and unyielding hard work. But beyond the success, his true legacy is in the lives he touched, the values he instilled, and the inspiration he leaves behind for those who follow. His story is more than one of success; it's a reminder that with courage, perseverance, and a heart for others, anyone can rise above their circumstances. As he steps forward, his legacy of integrity, generosity, and family will continue to echo.

About the Ghost Author

It's not every day that you have the opportunity to ghostwrite a book. But this year, I have had both the honor and privilege to capture the business life stories of one of the most incredible men I know, Floyd Davis.

This book was a collaborative effort between Floyd and me, serving as a testimony to how he reached where he is today.

By now, you know Floyd lived by many mottos, but this one rings loudest to me: *"I have never been afraid to try anything."*

***

I have known the Davis family since 1974.

I have a rich friendship with Floyd's daughters that spans decades now. I went to high school with Darcy and Shelly. We share many fond memories together from those years. Darcy and I were in the marching band together and graduated the same year. In recent years, we have enjoyed concerts, dinners, and a close friendship that has grown since our early high school days.

Shelly and I grew very close as we attended church together for many years. We have been prayer partners and prayer warriors for each other. Our children are within the same age range. They have been friends in youth groups and hung out together over the years. We have spent much time sharing and talking as lifetime friends.

Tonya and I developed a very close bond during a time of our lives when we were both single women raising our children. Our love and mutual support of one another have remained important anchors in our friendship—they are priceless.

I deeply cherish my friendship with Floyd's daughters. We have celebrated together and supported each other through life's challenges. I believe we have a sisterhood that I am confident will carry us years into our future.

Floyd's son, Calvin, was a few years younger than me. I attended church with him and his wife, Andrea, only a few years before his early, unexpected death. He was a kind young man, just like his father.

Floyd and Angela, who was affectionately known as Grangie, offered me the opportunity to serve as their family photographer at many recent family gatherings. This has afforded me the privilege to personally know this large, loving family Floyd is most proud of.

As the book's ghostwriter, my hope is that you have enjoyed the compelling stories on each page, and as a dear friend of the family, I also hope that you will be as amazed as I am at this man's dedication and his love for his family. I hope you have marveled at his accomplishments and been inspired by his grit, drive, and passion for life.

***

About the Ghost Author

In the final days of writing this book, I had the joy of joining Floyd and his daughters for his eighty-sixth birthday celebration lunch. I took the opportunity to ask him, "What would you say has been your greatest accomplishment?" Without any hesitation, he answered:

"MY GREATEST ACCOMPLISHMENT IS KNOWING WHEN I KICK THE BUCKET, SAY MY LAST FAREWELL, PASS TO OVER YONDER, I WILL DO SO KNOWING I'M LEAVING MY GIRLS, THEIR CHILDREN, MY GRANDCHILDREN AND MANY MORE DAVIS GENERATIONS AN ABUNDANCE FOR THEIR NEEDS TO BE TAKEN CARE OF. KNOWING IT WILL HELP MAKE THEIR LIVES BETTER. THAT'S PRETTY SATISFYING!!"

After working closely with Floyd for months now, I believe he would want to leave you with this:

"THERE'S NOTHING YOU CAN'T DO IF YOU PUT YOUR MIND TO IT AND PUT IN THE HARD WORK."

---

www.ingramcontent.com/pod-product-compliance
Lightning Source LLC
Chambersburg PA
CBHW070534090426
42735CB00013B/2977